SPLIT TICKET

Independent Faith in a Time of Partisan Politics

Amy Gopp, Christian Piatt,
Brandon Gilvin, eds.

ST. LOUIS, MISSOURI

Cover image: FotoSearch/Elizabeth Wright
Cover and interior design: Elizabeth Wright

Visit Chalice Press on the World Wide Web at
www.chalicepress.com

10 9 8 7 6 5 4 3 2 1 10 11 12 13 14 15

EPUB: 978-08272-34758 EPDF: 978-08272-34765

Library of Congress Cataloging-in-Publication Data

Split ticket : independent faith in a time of partisan politics / Amy Gopp, Brandon Gilvin & Christian Piatt, editors.

p. cm. — (WTF series)

ISBN 978-0-8272-3474-1

1. Christianity and politics. I. Gopp, Amy. II. Gilvin, Brandon. III. Piatt, Christian. IV. Title. V. Series.

BR115.P7S639 2010

261.7—dc22

2010008578

Printed in United States of America

Contents

SECTION THREE: We've Got Issues

OK; So here's the deal...

If you're like us, you've had plenty of "WTF?" moments with church and you asked one question.

No, not *that* one. Okay, maybe *that* one. At first. But that quick, flip question led to another, more important question: ***Where's The Faith?***

Faith in a God who can be present in both scripture and science. Faith that allows us to meet our neighbors on equal ground, no matter their ethnic, religious, or economic background. Faith that folks in their teens, twenties and thirties have something to contribute to the world, that they have big questions and big ideas about God, politics, sex, culture, the economy, justice, and what it means to be a human being.

We decided we wanted a series that brought as many young adult voices to the table as possible to talk in authentic, honest ways. These aren't slackers. They aren't overgrown adolescents. Instead of being talked about, or having questions posed about them, young adults are the ones framing the discussion, pushing the envelope, sharing their stories.

Discuss these stories amongst yourselves, or discuss them with us (series editors Brandon Gilvin and Christian Piatt) on Facebook on the WTF: Where's the Faith? page.

Read on.

Brandon and Christian

May God Make You Live in Interesting Times: An Introduction

My Bosnian friends always wish the best for me. Each time I leave my adopted homeland of Bosnia and Herzegovina, they often look into my eyes and say, "May God make you live in interesting times." Bosnians have a way with words. In their uniquely poetic yet often discomfortingly direct way, they say it like it is. Their wish for me is actually an old proverb, one that has come true in more ways than they would probably care to admit.

"Interesting" can mean a lot of things—or mean nothing at all. In my friends' case, interesting has far too often meant their neighbors turning against them; finding themselves trapped in the valley of their cosmopolitan capital city and surrounded by armed men they used to call their friends; running for their lives to collect water in recycled soda bottles so they could choose between flushing the toilet or taking a sponge bath; regaining a sense of normalcy after one of the most bloody, brutal, and baffling wars in recent history.

Interesting enough?

Having lived there during and after the Bosnian War (1992—1995), I returned to the United States in 1999. For the past ten years I have regularly traveled back to the region of the former Yugoslavia, accompanying many delegations from my church denomination, conducting further research on how humans can coexist, especially in a pronounced interfaith context, and performing with my beloved interfaith choir in Sarajevo.

I have witnessed—albeit peripherally—how a formerly socialist government has slowly and painstakingly taken baby steps toward embracing capitalism. Some might call it democratic. So far, I am not yet convinced. Nor am I convinced that democracy is the end-all-be-all. Democracy remains a project, a work in progress. An experiment in making choices that often ends up being partisan and divisive.

Democracy is an experiment?

Democracy is an experiment for us too, as is one of its main components: religious tolerance and "freedom." Both are concepts we certainly aspire to but rarely achieve.

Even though many of us in North America rarely question the concept, the democratic system is still, in the whole scope of human existence, a trial. We haven't gotten it right yet, not that we ever will. We certainly are making bigger strides than baby steps, but we're participating in a detailed, ongoing, complex process.

After all, it only took us a couple of centuries to elect someone who is not part of the dominant culture to a position that truly matters. I wonder how long it will take before we muster enough courage to elect a female to the most prestigious office on earth. Then again we're still fighting with the powers-that-be for the right to choose what to do with our own bodies. We are just now putting on our gloves to face those who would stand in the way of, or even take away, our right to make a public, legal, lifelong vow to the ones we love. As those persons stand in our way, we stand in solidarity with the thousands upon thousands who have been snuffed out before their time, thanks to our own government's trained killers—all in the name of national freedom, security and, dare I say, democracy.

Interesting enough?

I vividly remember being told by a member of my home congregation that politics had no place in our faith, and vice-versa. The sermon I preached that morning a decade or so ago was apparently too "political" (some used the word "challenging"). Naïve and prone to people-pleasing, I also vividly recall second-guessing myself, wondering why I always insisted on calling things as I saw them. Most of the time that meant acknowledging and naming the injustice and oppression I witnessed in our world. A sermon most folks in my church labeled as "political" was actually highlighting the actions Jesus took to embody love in a world of fear.

We're still experimenting.

But for so many, our North American, predominantly white, middle-class, "hardworking" Puritan ethic (coupled with an immature fervor that the American dream is truly reachable by all) means the difference between life and death. Tragically death has more consistently prevailed. And it's our hands that are bloody.

So here we are, searching to live out our faith expressed by the many Christianities present in our current U.S. context. And we are striving to do so in an increasingly globalized and pluralistic world where there is more partisanship, division, backbiting and intolerance than anyone confessing to follow Christ would care to admit. We are young adults living only a decade into this new millennium.

The words you will read on the pages to follow are the stories of young adults in our 20s and 30s expressing our religious and spiritual beliefs and political convictions at a time when partisan politics rule and faith can come across as all too independent, fundamentalist (whether on the "left" or "right"), or irrelevant. But I trust you will also find in our stories some models for action and hope, even though we are not all on the same page.

We may be a split ticket at times, but our generation may also be the one to lead us all to that place where unity can, indeed, be found in our beautiful, messy, frustrating, and fascinating diversity.

I believe this collection points us to two notions: No position is apolitical, and all human beings have guiding principles in their lives that give them the means by which to make sense of life.

Even those in our midst who claim to be atheists or agnostics—the questioning, the seeking, the critical, the confused, the pissed-off, and the organized religion-rejecters—even they are not without faith. In my experience, they are often the ones with the most courage to challenge the *status quo*.

My self-proclaimed atheist friend Nada, who stood next to me in the soprano section of my Bosnian interfaith choir, taught me that singing sacred music with persons of other ethnicities was not about faith as much as it was a political statement. When we human beings want to, we can find it within ourselves to come together and lift our voices in songs of solidarity and peace, regardless of what motivates us to do so.

Our spiritual lives cannot be extracted from our daily experiences. Our civic lives—whether we're the pawns in someone else's political game or the ones in charge—are also part of who we are as sacred beings with creative natures and spirits. In the end, we all walk in mystery on this earth. We all yearn to live lives of dignity.

As we awaken to new opportunities to become actors on the world's stage, we continue to struggle to find God in the voting booth. Perhaps we deny that God is already there, or we do not vote at all. Perhaps we take down the dominant systems and structures that serve death instead of life, finding that we can come together in faith—however each of us individually defines that—just as we have to figure out how to be citizens of our own respective governments and inhabitants on Earth.

Empowered then, we may look into one another's eyes and say, "May we continue to live in interesting times." Inspired, we go into the world as change agents moving with God, wishing, working and indeed hoping the best for humanity. We move undaunted by the capriciousness of that word, "interesting."

Amy Gopp

SECTION ONE

From Awakenings to Activism

Greg Turk

1

Hearing Music through the Silence

The band exploded on a sunny day in Los Angeles, forcefully sending Mexican *Banda* music out and upward. There were only three of them: a bouncing tuba player, a booming bass drummer, and a wailing trumpet, but they were loud, demanding that they be heard. It was the sound one might expect for a parade, streets lined with kids grasping cotton candy, perched on parent's shoulders, and watching as the music neared.

Instead, the scene was that of a funeral for Miguel. He had just turned twenty, become a father, and started a new job. A young man from a beautiful yet gang-ridden neighborhood of South Central Los Angeles whose hope recently had begun outshining his despair.

The band's playing signaled to Miguel's father and two brothers, one older and one younger, to grab shovels, standing like empty crosses in the ground, and begin throwing dirt on the casket. As they threw the dirt to cover up death, I stood there in my robe, feeling the powerful defiance of the band. They played for a crying mother and family, sobbing friends, "homeboys" trying their best to hold in emotion, and more. Beyond the immediate audience, the band filled the deep blue sky with the sound of horns, drums, and cymbals to declare that the violent death of

Miguel would not go unnoticed. They played so that somehow, all our human brothers and sisters would hear the cry for new life as the music ascended toward God.

At the time I had been pastor of All Peoples Christian Church for about five years, and presiding over a Catholic funeral was new to me. While a "just in case" priest was present to make sure it was really Catholic, I felt honored in my role, especially since I had enjoyed a year of a wonderful and blessed relationship with Miguel. He had come looking for a job and a changed life at All Peoples, a congregation of extraordinarily gracious and loving people sharing life and a building with "the Center." The Center is a multiservice agency called All Peoples Christian Center, a powerful agent of change and good led by longtime drum major Saundra Bryant.

All Peoples rose, "like a phoenix from ashes" as the congregation likes to say, in response to the injustice of imprisoning Japanese Americans during World War II. On All Peoples' campus was The Japanese Christian Institute until it was left vacant as its members were arrested and interned around the country. Dan and Frances Genung traveled in 1942 to 822 E 20th Street, beginning a new ministry of the Christian Church (Disciples of Christ) called All Peoples Christian Church.

This ministry would later multiply to include a nonprofit agency, All Peoples Christian Center, in a successful effort to increase its impact in this highly impoverished community. Around 2003 the Los Angeles Police Department's Newton Division, where All Peoples is located, estimated that sixty-six gangs with more than 12,000 gang members were living in that relatively small area. These communities often experienced some of the highest murder rates in the city.

The band kept playing as dirt covered the casket, and I thought, *enough is enough*. I had grown tired of that phrase. I had started a "ministry of hanging out" in South Central, as I had done in other cities. It placed high value on intentionally establishing and wandering into relationships where people are, in order to provide a loving and gracious relational space. In the case of gang members, it meant going to streets, porches, hospitals, funerals, and jails. This incarnational style of ministry doesn't wait for folks to come to me; rather, it invites me to go to be with them in order to represent—and re-present—Gospel love and grace as best I can. This ministry gave me with an ever-expanding circle of relationships by which I, along with All Peoples, could encounter and serve people in their need.

Miguel came for a job at Homie Accents, our specialty soap microenterprise that provided support to gang members seeking change. His quick success led him to full-time employment elsewhere. Miguel's "new life" made him and those around him proud. Both his mother and fiancé expressed their joy with tears as they had greater confidence that he'd come home safe on any given day.

To celebrate and share his excitement, Miguel attended a party out of the neighborhood with some geographically distant homeboys. Three young men walked into the party and opened fire, shooting seven and killing four. When the paramedics arrived, Miguel was one of the dead.

While dirt continued to be thrown into the hole to a Mexican tune, my mind drifted to a scene from a few years earlier when I sat on a curb outside the housing projects of LA's Boyle Heights, a nearby community equally familiar with gang violence. Grandparents, parents, and children of the community broke from their Saturday morning routines and gathered along with others from near and far to participate in a march from "the projects" to the Los Angeles County Jail, a symbol for the local judicial system. All came to be heard in their stance against California State Proposition 21.

Proposition 21

Proposition 21 was placed on the California ballot in 2000 as an attempt to stem youth violence. Among other things, it took the complex judicial issues of the court to the public in an effort to "mega-legislate" harsher treatment for juvenile offenders. According to the League of Women Voters, proposed changes to juvenile and adult law would move more juvenile offenders to trial in adult court, requiring certain young offenders to be held in local or state correctional facilities. It would increase penalties for gang-related crimes and expand the list of violent and serious offenses warranting longer sentences. The legislation, according to Daniel B. Wood of *The Christian Science Monitor* (March 9, 2000) positioned prosecutors rather than judges as the authorities to decide whether fourteen-year-old and older juveniles would be tried in adult court. Those arguing for Prop.21 felt that "tougher" sentencing with wider breadth was a way to protect the public from youth crime.

The argument against Prop.21 was that these youth could already be tried as adults in California and that the massive cost of the legislation—and resulting detention costs—for correctional departments could be better allocated toward prevention efforts to lessen violence. They believed that the proposition was bad policy that fed on public fear, and that the proposition would negatively affect communities.

The Faith to Cultivate and Hold a Vision

Early in Jesus' ministry, on a Saturday, perhaps as beautiful as the day of Miguel's funeral or the gathering in the projects of Los Angeles, Jesus and the disciples walked together through a grain field as they made their way to the synagogue. In the fields, they plucked the heads of grain (Mark 2:23). Doing so, they were confronted by some Pharisees saying, "Look, why are they doing what is not lawful on the Sabbath?" (v. 24). This had become a theme for Jesus, as his behavior had inspired local authorities to question him repeatedly. These experiences informed the disciples as they plucked and ate, gaining attention for Jesus', and now their, behavior as they broke the law on the Sabbath. Jesus responds, saying "The Sabbath was made for humankind, and not humankind for the Sabbath; so the Son of Man is lord even of the Sabbath"(vv. 27–28).

The vision we hold of the future is critically important. It is the end, or *telos,* to which we are oriented, and it greatly influences our daily perspective and action. For instance, many hold a clear image of a house at Christmas. December arrives, and creativity and energy to decorate increase as resources and time are found to complete the "goal." Action is taken, and lo and behold, the activity brings the vision of the house into reality. Try to get someone who holds such a picture to *not* decorate at Christmastime and it will most likely bring a strong response. The dominant picture we hold of the future—even if projected from our past—moves us to expend energy and creativity to find ways

> the vision we hold of the future is critically important.

to actualize it. To allow God to inform what we foresee permits a faithful vision for that which we're to cocreate.

Plenty of people are willing to tell us what is "realistic" as they interpret what they believe are possibilities for a person, a community, the human family, now and tomorrow. However, it is essential that our vision not be limited by others' interpretations of what is realistic in order to allow the freedom to see and feel in our imagination that for which God longs. As children may see and feel Christmas morning before Dec. 25—the vividness of vision and the attraction of constructive emotion attached—it can move them to change behavior.

We are to see and feel that which we're called to cocreate with God in a way that awakens us from our current reality and causes us to run to make it so with that same sense of excitement, anticipation, and urgency.

The cultivation of a faith-filled vision has competition. Some are subtle but strong, such as the mechanisms and levers for socialization that teach and influence dominant morals and laws of the land. These include school, family, law enforcement, and even faith communities. As Jesus bumps into these, he appears to be working from a different script than what is accepted by those in power around him. While social structures are necessary and valuable, they are not God, nor are they permanent. Jesus illustrates this in his response to being called out for breaking the law on the Sabbath by asserting that the Son of Man is lord of the Sabbath.

*SOCIAL STRUCTURES ARE NOT GOD

His actions are influenced by a higher view, which the disciples are to "catch," of how people and community are to exist in relationship, subordinating social norms, and even laws, as variables. Existing within present structures to maintain a current reality is secondary to faithfully cocreating the world as God would have it. The disciples' experience with Jesus informs them of this vision. The task of their faith is more than believing (even the demons believe). It includes "seeing" with vision that which is not yet and faithfully acting in accordance with that vision.

All Peoples had experienced injustice and the ugliness of the world in very personal ways, both individually and collectively. These experiences inspired them to courageously establish a vision filled with hope. They are convinced that current reality is not how it must always be, and they see that which will replace it. The vision they hold is communicated through worship, Bible study, conversation, and daily action as they are certain that God is making all things new, and that we are coresponsible for cocreating with God an "earth, as it is in heaven." The members of All Peoples are fully aware of existing brokenness and injustice, but this brokenness is overwhelmed by vision that moves them to speak and act to bring change.

It is from within this band of faithful visionaries that I saw in my heart and mind the streets of South Central with grandmothers playing ball with grandchildren, grandfathers laughing and joking while kids jump rope on sidewalks, teens buoyant with hope and excited about the future, and peace, sweet peace, swirling throughout. I could see and feel it, although I looked around and was confronted by a current reality that did not match the vision. The dominance of the vision compelled us to join in a vision-building activity, such as meeting on the corner in the projects as we awaited a march.

The common theme of the group gathered on the river of pavement in the shadows of downtown L.A. was not only that this is not how life is supposed to be; it was expressly projecting a vision of something more, especially for the children and youth of the community. Projecting a faithful vision of life without the desperation of poverty and inadequate educational and social systems, and without youth living out suicidal tendencies in homicidal ways. That picture was replaced with one of shared peace and prosperity, a supportive and nurturing educational and social system, and young people who are hopeful and healthy. The vision was palpable. The "yes" to the vision outweighed the "no" of the current reality, dismissing any apathetic tendencies and compelling action. It was happening!

Vision-Inspired Action

Starting in the projects of Boyle Heights, east of downtown, the march was a striking visual commentary as poor, mostly Latino folks moved across one of the old bridges over the Los Angeles River. These bridges hold many stories from the past of Mexican Americans walking to and from gardening and housekeeping jobs on the "west side." The bridges symbolize a segregation and racism that bully their way into the present. The hundred and fifty marchers were doing something to speak and act on their vision, to make it real, now, with signs and banners, drums, and singsong calls for a better life for their community, its youth, and thereby the whole of Los Angeles.

Nobody knew the effects of gang violence more intimately than this community. In Boyle Heights, as in the neighborhood around All Peoples, funerals for young people were commonplace. To suggest that everyone was affected would be a sad understatement, as everyone was repeatedly affected by violence. So the cry against tougher laws wasn't a desire for being soft as much as it was a desire for solution, a new normal. It is generally agreed that "Getting tough on crime" as a primary legal strategy has not worked in Los Angeles with gang violence. It is hard to threaten effectively those who have no hope.

Sometimes people would ask me, "Don't gang members realize that their choices will only lead them to prison, drug-addicted death, or death by violence?" I told them that the problem isn't that they don't know; they *do* know. They know how powerful hopelessness is. That's why the march, the cocreating of a here-and-now where faith, hope, and love reign was such an important call heard that day. We moved across the bridge and toward the skyscrapers on top of one of the wealthiest plots of land in the world.

When Jesus and the disciples entered the synagogue on a Saturday, Jesus acted. A "broken" man with a withered hand was there among the people, and they watched to see if Jesus would cure him, "…so that they might accuse him" (Mark 3:2). Jesus called the man forward, from the margins of those gathered and asked, "'Is it lawful to do good or to do harm on the sabbath, to save life or to kill?' But they were silent" (v.4).

The marchers were not silent as their heartfelt vision moved their feet, hands, and voices to act. With no multimillion dollar marketing budget for television ads, or the political or economic clout to convene meetings in the skyscrapers that cast shadows over them as they marched, people acted according to their vision to make way in the present for God's future. They acted to cocreate a system that prevents violence, heals lives, and brings a new normal to broken people and communities.

By the time I was called to All Peoples I had worked with gang members for about eight years in other cities. In all that time, it was confirmed for me that this is where I belonged, out of my own need as much as anything. One of the things I learned and grew to appreciate greatly was the emphasis on action. In fifteen-plus years of that work, I have never had someone ask for my educational or professional credentials. They have not wanted to know what political stances I took or the groups to which I belonged. They have wanted to know who I was on that day and what I was doing.

All Peoples was very similar in its action-oriented approach to faith. During the campaign against Proposition 21, it became a hub of organizing activity, not for the purpose of being politically active, but for the purpose of being faithful. Worship and prayers, conversation and study, pats on the back and copying fliers were all actions bursting with vision, as were organizing efforts such as gathering two busloads of people to join in a downtown protest.

A hopeful vision isn't just a wish. Rather, it compels us to wake up to potentials, and then to act to make the vision so. Marginalized people need vision acted on far more than they need great ideas with no action.

Space to Reflect

Having walked a couple of miles from the projects, through the shadows of downtown L.A., we arrived at L.A. County's Men's Central Jail, part of a system that normally holds 20,000 to 25,000 inmates on a given day. Grandmothers with grandchildren, fathers with daughters, "activists," ex-gang members, and more assembled on a small piece of grass on the corner of Bauchet and North Vignes Streets.

In the synagogue, standing with the man with the withered hand, Jesus presented the worshiping body with a question, "… to save life or to kill?"(v.4). The response of silence moved him to anger, and he grieved that they'd lost a heartfelt urge to act with love to bring another to wellness. Jesus acted to heal the man. "The Pharisees went out and immediately conspired with the Herodians against him, how to destroy him" (v.6).

Standing, packed into that patch of grass, with grandmothers and children, teenagers and organizers, we watched as the Sheriff's Department send forty to fifty deputies to march around us in full riot gear. We had a permit to be there for thirty minutes, which, I imagine, is how they knew to expect us. With dark helmets and protective masks, batons in hand, and additional riot gear hanging from belts, they marched back and forth in a demonstration of force. They were clearly trained not to look at us, at least not directly.

I remember the look on the face of a woman, maybe 70 years of age, as we stood near one another. She drew a young girl to her side, and I imagined her mind drifting back to another place and time, when soldiers of another country made it clear that they could crush their citizenry if they so chose.

The gathering wasn't long-lived. We came and went as law-abiding citizens, walking back peacefully. The return across the bridge was less vocal and organized, more like a walk home from church. The conversation, though, focused on assessing what happened, good and bad, and what we would do next. There was much to come.

1) Vision?
2) Act -
3) Reflect . . .

The reflection was in response to action, and held in context within the vision. It looked back and leaned forward to next strategic steps at the same time. All Peoples provided a place for reflection and strategy, often well into the night, to say "No to Prop.21" and "Yes" to a new vision. Christian congregations provide a natural space for such reflection, as the church says "Yes" to things not yet seen.

A Cycle: Vision, Act, Reflect

When the music stopped and the hole was filled, it was done, but not over. Embracing young homeboys with tears in their eyes, we knew that enough was enough. Sometimes I imagine the Los Angeles River's ceaseless stream through the city in a desert being composed of the tears of all the mothers of those killed by gang violence. Just a week prior, with Miguel's strides forward, his mother enjoyed some comfort in the thought that her son would come home alive on any given day. Sadly, the last time he came home was in a casket for an all-night vigil in their apartment. Her tears flowed, as had so many others before hers and far too many since. I don't know if they've ever stopped. Walking across the grass on that Saturday, I thought back to the other Saturdays, the activities around Proposition 21 and Jesus in the synagogue.

Proposition 21 passed, and today, a few years later, the state is scrambling to deal with overcrowded prisons, the excessive financial demands they place on the California budget, and the need for more effective ways to "deal with" violent crime. The Los Angeles police chief and Los Angeles County sheriff now include in their statements that we "cannot arrest our way out of this problem." Suppression and harsher treatment haven't provided a solution, nor did they intervene in the life of the "shooter" to save Miguel or ease the pain of grief endured by his loved ones. That such homicides regularly occur in Los Angeles County has become accepted as normal.

For the disciples, it was likely clear that Jesus was not "normal," nor was he content to repeat patterns that maintained the current norm. His transformational acts of faith had personal and social impacts and implications, even to the degree that powers and principalities felt threatened and pushed back. It is for those of us who look to Jesus as an example to be filled with a vision that allows us to see beyond that which is current reality and to act to draw that vision into the present as faithful agents of personal and social change.

The music stopped on that cemetery lawn. The hole was filled, but it is not over for Miguel, as God is bigger than life and death as we know it. And today, people seek to see and feel God's ever-swirling vision, compelling them to act, and strategically reflect in order to take next steps to cross a bridge under which tears no longer flow to a world where peace and justice and love-filled laughter is for all.

Questions for Discussion and Contemplation

1 Greg mentions "Homie Accents," a microbusiness that helps former gang members redevelop their skills. How might your faith community think "outside the box" to engage a social issue in your neighborhood?

2 Do you think that there is any crime that warrants a juvenile being considered as an adult in the criminal justice system? What circumstances might call for that?

3 How might you implement the cycle of "Vision, Act, Reflect" in your own political activism?

Brian Dixon
Mary Sue Brookshire

2

Getting Engaged

In the beginning God created the heaven and the earth...And God saw every thing that he had made, and, behold, it was very good.
• Genesis 1:1, 31

"Attention! Draw swords! Genesis 1:1. Charge!"

Like all good Southern Baptist kids, we grew up hearing these words. Bible drills, along with memory verses and flannel boards, were staples of our early religious education. We—Mary Sue, born in Winston-Salem, North Carolina, and Brian, born three years later and hundreds of miles away in Winter Haven, Florida—began our lives of faith with these common experiences.

We both grew up in the South with working-class parents, all devoutly religious people committed to raising their children as Southern Baptists, but none of them all that interested in politics. In grade school, we spent almost as much time at church as we did at home or at school. While other kids were selling cookies and earning merit badges in Scouts for tying knots, we were earning patches as Royal Ambassadors and Girls in Action for writing to missionaries and building dioramas of Bible scenes in shoe boxes. We were the first in our families to go to college, and we both chose small, liberal arts, Baptist-affiliated institutions and got involved in on-campus religious organizations.

In 1996, in our first year of seminary in Atlanta, our paths finally crossed. We actually met before school even started, in the graduate student housing office. On move-in day, while everyone else was unpacking boxes and getting settled, Brian, sporting the cheesiest mustache east of the Mississippi, bounced up to the desk to return his *promptly* completed interest survey (the only interest survey returned on move-in day, or *any* day for that matter). There to receive it was Mary Sue, graduate resident director, clad in her favorite denim overalls, the same overalls she was wearing when Brian and his mustache came walking into Old Testament 101 three days later. A friendship was born.

During the daily shuttle bus rides to and from campus, we chatted and got to know each other, discovering just how much we had in common. "*You* love sausage biscuits? *I* love sausage biscuits! *You* love Jeopardy? ME TOO!" In fact, we learned we had just missed meeting one summer at a beachside Baptist camp. Eventually Mary Sue invited Brian to come to church with her, the Baptist church, where over the next several years we practiced being ministers, serving as deacons, working with the youth, and teaching Sunday school. And it was there, within two weeks of each other, that we both knelt to receive the laying on of hands as we were ordained to Christian ministry.

After we graduated from seminary, neither of us really wanted to leave Atlanta, so we both took jobs at the same university and became roommates. Despite our insistence to the contrary, some people remained convinced that we were a couple and often treated us as such. We even started to get joint invitations to friends' weddings (about which we agreed, "One invitation, one gift, suckah!"). Although we weren't romantically involved, we acted a lot like an old married couple, taking ballroom dance classes, hosting Tupperware parties, and cooking our favorite meals together.

After four years as roommates, we were both surprised to find ourselves moving to California—another major life event, like our ordinations, within two weeks of each other. Neither of us ever imagined we'd leave sweet tea, biscuits and gravy, or other staples of our life in the South. But leave we did. Brian relocated to San Francisco to begin his first call as pastor of a small Baptist church, and Mary Sue sold most of what she owned and drove her Honda to San Diego to be with the love of her life.

That was five years ago. We've been friends now for over ten years, and the list of things we have in common continues to grow. As new California converts, we both love the double cheeseburgers at In 'N Out, we can't stand temperatures below 60 degrees, and we can't believe an action hero is our governor. But with all these things in common, we are different in one significant way: Mary Sue can, and did, marry the person she loves. Brian, because he is gay, is denied that right.

With so much connecting us, we never thought anything could make us feel separate. But with the passage of Proposition 8, the measure revoking the right of same-sex couples to marry, we felt disconnected in a way we never had.

Brian

> And a voice came from heaven, 'You are my Son, the Beloved; with you I am well pleased.' (Mark 1:11)

I had never felt this alienated before. "I'm mad at all straight people today," I ranted to Mary Sue. Not because I believed all straight people had voted for Proposition 8—I knew that wasn't true because Mary Sue had worked tirelessly to defeat it—but instead because straight people had a right that I didn't have. I hadn't ever really felt discriminated against because of my sexuality. Up to that point I never really felt that being gay made me that different from anyone else. I was, after all, a white male. Let's face it, being white and being male often presented me with a great deal of privilege.

As we said above, I grew up in a moderate Baptist family in the middle of Florida. We didn't talk about sex in our family. We *still* don't talk about sex in my family. To this day my parents have never had "the talk" with either me, my brother, or my sister. (My brother and sister both have children, so I think they probably figured it out.) As a teenager, I chalked my lack of interest in girls up to being a good Baptist boy. Honestly, I didn't even really know what "gay" was. But after three months of fooling around with my college roommate, I thought perhaps something made me different.

I finally came out of the closet about three months before I entered seminary. Much to my surprise I found that seminary and the church I joined were both welcoming to and affirming of gays and lesbians. But even if I hadn't found such an open church or seminary, I don't believe that I would ever have had the internal faith struggle that many people have. I'm not sure why but I'm really grateful that I never questioned whether or not I was exactly who God created me to be. I believed the words from the Bible that I had been taught. Words like "and God said that it was good"; "for God so loved the world"; and "you are my beloved." I did spend four years after seminary looking for a call where I could be out, but part of that time was really spent figuring out where I wanted to go and what I wanted to do. When I received a call to pastor a church, it was in San Francisco, where I'm not looked at strange because I'm gay but because I'm a minister or Baptist. All in all I've lived my life pretty openly, never feeling any discrimination as a result of my sexuality and never feeling as if I was being denied any of my rights.

18,000 Weddings= ONE BIG PARTY

There was so much excitement all over the state and the country, when California began issuing marriage license to same-sex couples. Ceremonies were being held everywhere, and over 18,000 couples were married—vows exchanged, cakes eaten, champagne corks popped. I had the privilege of officiating at two of these weddings. It felt as if we were in the middle of one giant party. But underneath all the jubilation was a growing anxiety, a fear that as quickly as this right had been granted it would be taken away. Many feared that Proposition 8 would pass, but I was never one of them. I couldn't imagine that California of all places would ever pass such a law. I expected such action in the "Bible Belt," where I had lived, but surely not on the "left coast" that is often vilified throughout the rest of the country as being too "liberal." I just couldn't imagine that I personally would ever have my rights revoked. I wasn't just saddened when Proposition 8 passed; I was shocked.

I also felt incredible guilt. I hadn't done enough.

* I hadn't done enough

I had invited people from the "No on 8" campaign to come to the church I pastor and I had gone to an interfaith service in support of same-sex couples, but that was it. Compared to many—*compared to Mary Sue*—I had done very little. I hadn't made any phone calls, I hadn't attended any rallies, and I hadn't given any money. And still worse I hadn't spoken to my family about how important this issue was to me. Most of my family lives in Florida, where a similar proposition passed. Just as it was when we skipped "the birds and bees" chat, we still weren't talking about sexuality. I didn't make it clear how if they voted for the proposition in their state they were voting to take away my—their son's—rights. I hadn't made clear how important it was to me. Perhaps I didn't know how important the right to marry was to me until the right was taken away.

The first few days post-Proposition 8 were difficult. I didn't want to leave the house because I didn't want to have to look people in the eyes who might have voted to take away my rights. Much was being made about the high percentage of African Americans and Latinos who had come out to vote for Barack Obama but who had also voted in higher numbers, proportionately, for Proposition 8. Whether those initial percentages were accurate or not, I felt betrayed by the very people for whose inclusion I had often worked. In an election that seemed to break down so many barriers, another barrier was becoming more apparent. I wanted to celebrate the election of Barack Obama. I wanted to celebrate the historic nature of that occasion. I wanted to celebrate the fulfillment of a promise in our country that you really can do and be anything you dream. But I couldn't celebrate because I knew that wasn't true. It wasn't true for everyone. It wasn't true for me.

Mary Sue

> God is love, and those who abide in love abide in God, and God abides in them…There is no fear in love, but perfect love casts out fear. (1 John 4:16, 18)

When I called Brian on November 5, the day we learned that Prop.8 had passed, I was afraid. I didn't know what to say. There was no way, as a married woman, I could express my deep grief to my dearest friend without feeling conspicuously guilty. I had something he had just been denied. I knew that even my most heartfelt sentiments would ring slightly hollow. I wasn't surprised when Brian told me he was mad at all straight people that day, but I was hurt. Not by Brian, but by the awareness that for the first time, something had come between us. I was hurt, and I was angry. Angry because it felt like hate had won, hate masquerading as piety and righteousness. Angry because I had been more politically active than ever, and it wasn't enough.

I'm sad to say that I'm usually one of those people cruising along that dreaded road, the one paved with good intentions. It's not that I don't care about things. I do. I care about the environment, about Darfur, about breast cancer. I just never seem to translate my concerns into meaningful action. That is, until last year, when I got involved in the fight to defeat Prop.8. And I'm not really sure what got me off my duff this time. Part of it was that many of the people I love most in this world are gay. Part of it was that I was a new mother, and I felt a responsibility to help create the kind of world I want for my children.

But I think the biggest reason I finally got active was that I realized my political beliefs and my faith could not be separate. I had to stand up to people who were using the Bible to cut people off from their basic human rights. I had to stand up for what I had been taught in that Southern Baptist Sunday school class: that God is love, and that those who abide in love abide in God.

My political beliefs and my faith could not be separate.

While other people were beginning the work to defeat Prop. 8, I was figuring out how to be a mother to twins, so I came late to much of the effort. At my first clergy organizing meeting in September, I picked up a handful of bumper stickers and a yard sign. Driving into our neighborhood, I was keenly aware of how lonely my "No on 8" sign would be on our street. As I walked out into our yard to plant my sign in the soft earth, my pulse quickened. I was afraid. What would my neighbors think? What might they do? But with the fear came the reminder that Love was surrounding me, and I felt as alive in my faith as I ever had.

After that first meeting, I jumped headlong into the fight against Prop.8. I made calls at a clergy phone bank event; I donated money for the cause; I protested outside a local church hosting a "Yes on 8" rally; I spoke at an interfaith worship service one afternoon and performed my first gay wedding that same night. And on Election Day, I volunteered to work the polls for the campaign, making one last effort to encourage people to vote against Proposition 8.

I woke up at 5:00 a.m. on November 4 to a rare cold and rainy day in San Diego. I helped my husband feed our children and then I reported to the designated meeting place for my assignment. In California just about any location can be a polling place, and I was assigned to a one-car garage in a residential neighborhood. By the time we marked off the legally required distance we had to keep away from the polling place, it became clear that we would not be able to talk with many voters. In the rain, people parked close by and didn't even have to walk past us. Without an umbrella, I stood for hours in the rain, feeling useless and frustrated.

That feeling only intensified as the election results began to come in.

The day after the election, I felt dejected, defeated, and depressed. Even the celebration over Barack Obama's victory, for which I was grateful, felt painful and disingenuous. All the comments about "how far we have come" on the road toward equality felt so hypocritical in the face of the passage of Prop. 8 and similar legislation in other states. When will we learn?

But what troubled me most—what I found downright infuriating and despicable—was that so many of the arguments put forth by the "Yes on 8" campaign were distortions of the truth, aimed at generating fear in otherwise thoughtful citizens. Pastors stirred up their congregations by declaring that if Prop.8 didn't pass, all ministers would be required to perform gay weddings. Simply not true. In commercials for Prop.8, cameras panned in on the sad faces of children, imploring voters to remember them as they cast their votes, falsely claiming that if Prop.8 were defeated, teachers would be required to teach the virtues of gay marriage to young schoolchildren.

Proponents of Prop.8 wanted people to be afraid, and sadly, it worked.

At a press conference after the interfaith worship service I participated in, a reporter asked me if I thought my fellow Christians who were proponents of Prop.8—thousands of whom were gathered at that moment at a huge prayer rally at our local football stadium—were hateful people. "I think fear makes people do hateful things," I replied. "And I think those people are afraid. But what we are talking about here today is love, and perfect love casts out fear." In the days after the election, I wanted so desperately for that to be true. And I prayed that God would take away my own fear, the fear that the world will never change, the fear that Brian and I were now separate in a way we had never been.

fear makes people do hateful things.

Brian and Mary Sue

> "There is no longer Jew or Greek, there is no longer slave or free, there is longer male and female; for all of you are one in Christ Jesus." (Galatians 3:28)

The passage of Prop.8 and the heartbreak it caused us both gave us our first real sense of our separation. But paradoxically it also brought us together, reminding us that in Christ Jesus, we are one. Despite our differences, we both spent most of the days following the passage of Proposition 8 feeling belittled, angry, guilty; we stewed over what happened, what others did or didn't do, and what we had failed to do as well.

Then came the weekend. Tensions had been building all week, and with those tensions people began organizing—through Facebook, MySpace, Twitter, and blogs—getting the word out any way they could. Marches and rallies were scheduled for the weekend. In San Francisco people would march on Friday night; in San Diego they would gather and march on Saturday. All over the country people were angry and they were taking to the streets. It was in these marches that we reconnected, 600 miles apart, at separate times, with different people.

As we marched, voicing our grief and our anger, we entered into a long tradition of protest that awakened us each to a sense of transformation.

* Re-connect

It was the first time Brian felt connected to all those folks who marched in Selma and Mobile and Washington D.C. Neither of us is old enough to have been a part of or even remember the civil rights movement led by Martin Luther King Jr. or John Lewis or Rosa Parks, but we were a part of this march and will remember this movement. Mary Sue knew at that moment that she would be able to tell her twins, Hannah and Isaac, that she stood up for their Uncle Brian's rights and perhaps even their rights.

At the same time, we also recognized that in this civil right movement, in these marches, we weren't being attacked by dogs and fire hoses, and the police weren't our enemies, but instead our protectors. As much as we could identify with those other marchers, their struggle would never be our struggle. But in our differences we were the same. We could all celebrate the victory of Barack Obama and what it symbolized. We could celebrate that a barrier was being broken down, that we were a step closer to the dream that Dr. King had.

We could also grieve the passage of Proposition 8. We could hold both of these contradictory emotions because we also remembered some other words of Dr. King, "Injustice anywhere is a threat to justice everywhere." Likewise any victory was not just a victory for the group receiving its rights but for all of us.

We've left much of that early Southern Baptist upbringing behind. But it's those early verses that we had to memorize, that we had to race to find in those Bible drills, that have sustained us and continue to teach us. In them we were and are told that we are good and beloved; that God is love and that perfect love casts our fear; that there is no longer Jew or Greek, male or female, black or white, gay or straight. It is in those same verses we hear "Attention! *Put Down* Swords!"

> They shall beat their swords into plowshares, and their spears into pruning hooks. (Isaiah 2:4)

Questions for Discussion and Contemplation

1 Have your friendships ever influenced your political commitments?

2 What role should the government play in regulating who gets to marry whom?

3 If your political affiliation is different from those held by your family, are there values, commitments, or other things that you have in common? What are they? Why?

4 What's the proper way for a faith community to be involved in a political process?

Amy Gopp

3

Holding Many Truths

Living out your faith often includes seeking the truth. Perhaps we will not find the "Truth" with a capital T, but certainly a truth, your truth, some sort of truth that allows us to make meaning out of our existence. In this age of partisan politics and the ever-declining Protestant Church as we know it, where do we find comfort in the truth?

> Pilate asked him, "So you are a king?" Jesus answered, "You say that I am a king. For this I was born, and for this I came into the world, to testify to the truth. Everyone who belongs to the truth listens to my voice." Pilate asked him, *"What is truth?"* (John 18:37–38)

Friar Ivo Markovic, a Bosnian Franciscan priest, and I traveled to the *Republika Srpska* (the Bosnian Serbian Republic) during the war in the former Yugoslavia. We met with the Bosnian Serb authorities at the Ministry of Religion. Not three minutes into our meeting, the authorities claimed that "Muslims are animals" and therefore not human. "They are Turks, part of the Ottoman Empire which defeated the Serbs on the Field of Blackbirds in 1389. They deserve to be wiped out!" exclaimed the Minister for Serbian Orthodox Religious Affairs.

As we drove away that day in Fra Ivo's car—with Croatian license plates—in enemy Serb territory after listening to such hatred, Ivo looked at me and said softly, "*Emica, ne brini se*—Amy, don't worry, hatred like this just *cannot* last."

And yet the summer of 1995, on July 11 to be exact, General Ratko Mladic and his Bosnian Serb forces surrounded the city of Srebrenica in Eastern Bosnia. In a little more than twenty-four hours, 8,000 Muslim men and boys were slaughtered. They were forced to evacuate their homes, lives, and all they once knew, all that was true and comfortable and safe. They were lied to, herded like cattle onto buses, trucks, and trailers and led to the battery factory on the outskirts of town. Once there, the men and boys were separated from the women and babies. They would never see each other again.

Thirteen years later we are still searching for the truth. Mothers, wives, daughters, and girlfriends, mistresses, grandmothers, and friends; we are still looking. Mass grave after mass grave has been discovered, but a mere 2,000 bodies or parts of bodies have been found. Suddenly "the truth" about someone's body is reduced to some arbitrarily quantifiable percentage. If seventy percent of the body parts can be proven as yours, you are buried and you receive a slim, green Muslim headstone with your name on it. Closure? A place for the living to revisit the dead? The missing? The terror? The truth? Is this all there is to show for the truth of 8,300 lives, senselessly slaughtered and practically forgotten by the rest of the world? Are these the god-awful Turks, the Ottomans who had defeated the Serbs now getting their due?

Fast-forward to 2002. CNN breaks the news that tapes from the Srebrenica massacres have been found and the truth about what happened on July 11, 1995, will finally be revealed. Zoom in now on my friend Ivona's family in the southern part of Herzegovina sitting around the obligatory coffee table in the center of their living room. Neighbors come over to drink the ubiquitous plum brandy, always offered in any proper Bosnian setting, and a cup of mud, a.k.a. Bosnian coffee. As they watch clips from CNN on the local Herzegovinian news, their Serb neighbors exclaim that they just can't believe how some people would be brainwashed into believing that these people on camera weren't just actors.

> Those aren't Muslims; that's just more Bosniak Muslim propaganda, supported by a pro-Western news channel, once again attempting to disavow the Serbian people of any power or authority. Can't people just accept the truth that the Serbian people were sent as those who would save Yugoslavia from itself? That we are the ones destined to lead our people—all of our people—back to the promised land of the socialist Tito years, where our national motto, "brotherhood and unity" said it all? Why is it just so hard to see the truth?

How does one ~~broker truth~~ build bridges?

How does one broker peace or build bridges in the face of such contending truths? Truths that cut to the core of peoples' identity, to the core of national, ethno-religious, and historical identity? How do we find the truth in history when history has, in and of itself, become ideology? How do we challenge and question revisionist history in the face of myriad complex social and cultural identities constructed as a result of the deep, deep pain of the past?

In a war zone, one learns to hold different versions of the truth at the same time. All at once, I as the outsider, the peace-builder, the pursuer of justice, and the bridge builder, had to grow into being comfortable handling and honoring many competing truths. At times I was a juggler just trying not to let one fall, at other times a laying hen protecting them all, and always a paranoid schizophrenic never quite sure which identity, which history, which truth would anxiously surface and express itself in some manner.

> Steadfast love and faithfulness [often translated as truth] will meet; righteousness [often translated as justice] and peace will kiss each other. (Psalm 85:10)

Love and truth and justice and peace will meet, promises the psalmist in that beautiful 85th Psalm, and truth will spring up from the ground. I think back to those mass graves in Srebrenica. The truth will indeed spring up from the ground. And I wonder what might happen when that truth is allowed to break in, to spring up, to step out and reach down into our souls as it motivates us to seek peace, pursue justice, and share love. I imagine that place perhaps to be reconciliation.

A year or two later, in the late '90s, Ivo and I made another trip to his childhood house: his birthplace. We traveled high into the mountains of central Bosnia until we arrived at a tiny village too small to be found on a map. Our first stop was at the Catholic (Croatian) cemetery, an overgrown piece of land no one seemed to tend. Ivo slowly made his way to the plots where eight of his male relatives were buried. In a deep, eerie, unavoidable silence, he stood in front of his father's grave to pay his respects and shed his tears. All eight men had been slaughtered only a couple of years before as innocent civilians by Muslim soldiers.

After leaving the cemetery we drove to the house where Ivo had been born and where his parents had lived their entire married life. With his father dead and his mother now a refugee in Croatia, Ivo made a point to visit the Muslim family that had occupied their family home. With no idea that their newly possessed house was Ivo's childhood home, they listened to his concern for their welfare in these new surroundings. They too had been expelled from their home in what is now the *Republika Srpska*.

Ivo ministered to these fellow victims of this dreadful war, offering his friendship, a listening ear, and words of comfort. He had met "the enemy"–those of the same ethnic group that had slaughtered his father–right there in his own home, and brought back their devastating truth and their human face. And I was his witness, working through my own preconceived notions, biases, and fears. As we returned to Sarajevo, we realized that we were not returning alone. We had the beautiful, suffering, familiar face of the enemy–now fellow human beings and children of God–with us.

* I say, "love your enemy"

Ivo's birthplace, a place where evil had resided during the war, had been transformed into a house of truth and reconciliation. For surely God lived there too.

While it was true that the Muslim troops ethnically cleansed the Croats and Serbs in that area of central Bosnia, every single person in that situation was a victim, every one of them bound together by the horrific circumstances that had turned their lives upside-down. The even deeper truth was that no one and nothing could change that we human beings are all undeniably connected one to the other, brothers and sisters, family of God. The Serbian Orthodox Christians and Croatian Roman Catholics, Bosniak Muslims and Sephardic Sarajevan Jews—all of them can trace their roots back to Abraham, Hagar, and Sarah.

We are all one in this circle of loving and living and suffering and dying. We are all touched by the Other, regardless of our political or religious persuasions.

truth is:
I. Living
II. Noun or verb?
III. Process
IV. Journey

Truth is a living, breathing entity. It is integrity, all things converging, consistent, cooperating, collaborating, and integrated. All things touching. The Latin root of the word "integrity" is probably *tangere*, which means "to touch." So the truth is about being touched, and it is the act of touching. When all things touch, all things are integrated, we are our truest selves. When we live from that deep source within, from a profound sense of knowing the truth of who we are at our lowest, our loneliest, our most vulnerable, our most naked; when we live from that source within, I believe we are in touch with what is the closest thing to what I can call the truth.

All I do, say, and believe comes from one source—the same place—the deepest, most intimate place within. Integrity is pursuing the life that God has called us to live, becoming the person God has brought us into being. Integrity is living the life we were meant to live. This is living the truth. And this truth does not adhere to any specific political party or any particular religious tradition. It is simply the truth of our existence, that which connects us all despite our best attempts at separation.

It is not some ethical belief or some certain moral position, and certainly not just an assemblage of facts; truth is in the way we live. It is not only a noun but also—and perhaps more accurately—a verb. It is something you do. Something you seek. It is not necessarily something you discover, and certainly not all at once. It develops. Truth is a process. Truth is a journey and a series of experiments.

Mahatma Gandhi spent many years of his life "experimenting" with truth. The greatest lessons of his life were precisely the questions that emerged from struggling, seeking, and standing up for the truth. But not even Gandhi was able to come to some sort of definitive conclusion about the truth, even with as much as he learned and knew.

In the film *Insignificance* (1985), director by Nicolas Roeg, the character named "The Professor", who evokes Einstein, puts it this way: "Knowledge isn't truth; it's just mindless agreement. You agree with me, I agree with someone else. We all have knowledge. We haven't come any closer to the truth. You can never understand anything by agreeing, by making definitions. Only by turning over the possibilities. That's called thinking. If I say I know, I stop thinking. As long as I keep thinking, I come to understand. That way I might approach some truth." Or, as the Psalm reads,

> You desire truth in the inward being; therefore teach me wisdom in my secret heart. (Psalm 51:6)

Shall we approach the Bible in much the same way? We often ask, "Are the scriptures true?" rather than "Can we find truth in the scriptures?" It doesn't matter what is true. What matters is the meaning we make, the meaning we come to construct. I don't care if Jesus was truly raised from the dead! I don't care! What matters to me is how that story speaks to my life as one who needs to resurrect each and every day. What matters to me is how that story speaks hope into the lives of those who confront death each and every day.

How are we going to live through the endless Good Fridays in our lives and make it through to Easter Sunday? How does the Gospel story fit into my story? Literalism or fundamentalism cannot take away the meaning we make of the biblical text, the stories that breathe new life into our own suffocating existence. For me, the women on the banks of the Babylon were the women of Bosnia, kicking and screaming as they were forced to sing a song to their captors in a foreign land. I would be a terrible member of the Jesus Seminar, I'm afraid.

But if we take seriously the text from John 14:6, *"I am the way, and the truth, and the life,"* we understand that to live the truth is to choose the way of the cross, the way of Christ, which is the way of love. There is nothing more profound than discovering that our life's deepest meaning is found in loving. For Christ to burst forth on the human scene as a way out of no way–as good news in the face of an oppressive Roman empire–was to claim that life can be found even in the midst of death and that God has revealed God's self to us through Jesus the Christ in flesh and bones.

When we have nowhere else to turn, when we are grasping for air, in over our heads, completely unclear about what is true, God kisses us on the forehead and tenderly whispers, *I love you, I love you, I love you…in you, I am well pleased, my child…this is the truth of your life. This is your greatest truth: that you have direct access to me, an intimate relationship with me is available to you…this is your way, may it inform your truth and your life all your days on the earth.*

The truth is liberating. It is a living, breathing entity. Truth is a form of beauty.

Some of the most intensely beautiful moments in my life have been spent singing in my interfaith choir in Sarajevo. "To sing is to pray twice," states an old proverb, eloquently capturing the mission of *Pontanima*. Our most earnest supplications have been the songs we have lifted up in the last decade. When we could rarely find the words to utter even the briefest prayer, we relied on our songs to speak to God and the rest of the world.

War has a way of leaving us speechless; music gives voice to those without words.

How else, in the midst of the immediate post-war context–our suffering Sarajevo under siege for so long–could we have sung the lilting lyrics of Bruckner's *Locus Iste*?

War leaves us speechless. Music gives us voice.

> *"This place made of God, inestimable mystery, is irreprehensible."*
>
> (loosely translated from the Latin)

Or the sincere and simple lines of the brilliant Mokranjac's *Tebe Poem*?

> *"We sing to You. We bless You. We give You thanks, Lord, and we pray to You, Our God."*
>
> (translated from the Old Slavonic)

The magic of music not only restored our personal prayers but also became our collective appeal for peace in a land ravaged, brutalized, and far too used to bloodshed. It was music–and only the transcendent truths expressed through music–that provided a reason for those from all ethno-religious backgrounds represented in Bosnia and Herzegovina to gather together twice a week. In those early years, when adequate food was still difficult to acquire and tramway tokens unaffordable for many, even under those circumstances music's invitation was too seductive.

To sing again was a summons to raise one's voice again. To be heard again. Undeniably, to sing was to live again and to express the truth of who you are. *Pontanima* extended this invitation.

We devoutly aspired to breathtaking eight-part harmonies, dramatic dynamics, and clear diction, but our overarching objective was to meet one another. Music was what brought us together, in all our diversity and vulnerability. And music sustained us even through the tensest moments, because *Pontanima's* invitation was not merely for individuals to lift their voices again, but also to enter into community.

I will never forget rehearsing the stunningly beautiful *Heruvimska pesma* for the first time. Not only did I have to decipher the Cyrillic alphabet; I had to capture the tender, haunting style of the Serbian composer. Singing each other's songs proved to be the most strategic step toward peace we ever could have made. To sing your enemies' songs is to confront that enemy and discover they too are only human. Uniting your voice with theirs makes real the call of the Hebrew prophet, Micah *"to do justice, and to love kindness, and to walk humbly with your God" (Micah 6:8).*

I believe that the encounter itself beckoned us forth, calling upon the very best of who we were as human beings and as lovers of Bosnia, regardless of whether we happened to be Orthodox, Catholic, Muslim, Mennonite, Jewish, Protestant, atheist, or questioning. The encounter during rehearsals, and more profoundly after rehearsals, over the ubiquitous and obligatory coffee, demanded we face the so-called "Other."

Even I, an Other, an outsider, an American who could never fully understand, was forced to face my own preconceived notions of who the Others were. A four-year volunteer with Mennonite Central Committee, I had accepted an invitation from Fra Ivo Marković to join him after he returned from his exile in Croatia back to Sarajevo. I was asked to help him found the Interreligious Peace Center "Face to Face" and to sing in the burgeoning choir. Little did I realize what that would mean for my life, my ministry, and my perspective of what is possible in the midst of so much that seems impossible. *Pontanima* deeply impacted not only my thinking but also my heart.

On a very intimate level, the choir became my family. I remember the laughter, sitting in the smoky basement of the Franciscan monastery, listening to the ostensibly endless *"Mujo and Sujo"* jokes. I remember perfecting the artistry and my own ability to make a rich, foamy pitcher of Bosnian coffee. I remember others–partners, spouses, friends, and family–who would join us after rehearsals so they too could be a part of our community. I remember the spontaneous singing, even after a laborious sacred music rehearsal, when someone would either break into *"Žuta Dunja"* or *"Bosna Moja"* (the song Ivo would incessantly try and teach me). And the serious party would begin if Marijo happened to be there with his bass or Željko with his guitar.

It was not unusual for me to climb up the hill ascending from *Baščaršija* to my apartment on *Toromanova ulica* in the wee hours of the morning. Every waking moment spent with my *Pontanima* family was worthwhile, memorable, and yet somehow commonplace. Perhaps that's the beauty of the choir, that it is based on the most ordinary stuff of life: relationships, communication, hard work, safety, and a sense of belonging. That the choir transcends all other groups we "belong" to is what makes it extraordinary.

On a professional level, it embodied the peace I was pursuing. Working closely with both Mennonites and Franciscans, the theology undergirding our peace-building was the foundation of the interreligious dialogue the choir so beautifully modeled. But when I think back on these nascent stages in the choir's history, I am amazed and proud of how organically it all developed. While a certain intentionality was definitely there, we never promoted the choir as an "interfaith project," but as a community that came together for a common purpose. The relationships that ensued were the natural by-products of the music we created together. Both songs and spirits were brought back to life.

For me, God's voice is the united voice of *Pontanima*, heard through the tenor velvet voice of my Muslim friend Miran harmonizing with the inimitable Orthodox bass voice of Dragan blending with the Catholic nun, Sister Slavica, singing alto and the sweet soprano voice of Zdenka. It is the voice of people trying to carry a tune and a message together, having to depend on each other's different tonalities, ranges, and breath while accepting each other's political and religious differences, quirks, pain, prejudice, and profound desire to be a part of something bigger than themselves.

Pilate asked, "What is truth?" He never waited for an answer. Instead, he turned to face the angry mob, hoping to release this King of the Jews. "I find no case against him. But you have a custom that I release someone for you at the Passover. Do you want me to release for you the King of the Jews?" (John 18:38–39)

We know how the story goes. That integrity to live one's life as truth itself, drawing upon the source of the living God that resides within each of us, in our guts, that most profound sense of knowing and to live and love from that place, even when it leads to conflict, upheaval, and death, that is living the truth. This is the way of Jesus the Christ.

> "You say that I am a king. For this I was born, and for this I came into the world, to testify to the truth. Everyone who belongs to the truth listens to my voice." (John 18:37b)

Questions for Discussion and Contemplation

1 How do you define "truth"? Are there ever multiple truths?

2 Have you ever been an outsider in a culture that was not your own? How did you deal with the differences? What made you uncomfortable? What was familiar?

3 What is the proper role for an outsider in working for change in a different culture?

4 Can you think of examples of when outside cultures have come in with intentions for positive change, but have had the opposite effect?

David Ball

[4]

Thy Revolution Come

An Invitation to Radical Discipleship

Hallowed Be Your Name...

> "When it is said that we disturb people too much by the words pacifism and anarchism, I can only think that people need to be disturbed, that their consciences need to be aroused, that they do indeed need to look into their work, and study new techniques of love and poverty and suffering for each other."
>
> • Dorothy Day, *The Catholic Worker*

The line of police stare grimly from behind the chain link fence, plastic handcuffs ready.

The names of the disappeared and dead—sung one by one in a haunting litany that stretches on and on for hours—are just audible beneath the roar of an army helicopter that dips lower and lower toward the crowd with every pass; these are only a few of our culture's martyrs. They are represented symbolically by people enacting a massacre draped in black and smeared in blood, lying at the entrance of this base responsible for training torturers, dictators, and assassins in Latin America. Many of their victims were church workers who took Jesus' message of love seriously enough to die for it.

The Western Hemisphere Institute for Security Cooperation (WHINSEC, formerly the School of the Americas or SOA), at Fort Benning, Georgia, founded to battle communism in the 1950s, has been implicated in many of the worst human rights abuses in Latin America's history. For those gathered at its gates, it symbolizes the oppression required to maintain our system of Empire and privilege, which puts the rule of money and law above human life, dignity, and respect for creation.

> *"Celina Ramos, 14 years old, El Salvador. Oscar Romero, archbishop of San Salvador. María del Carmen Idarraga de Gómez, Colombia."*

As our group of pilgrims approaches the fence, erected especially to keep the 20,000 annual participants out, a wall of military loudspeakers reminds us that we are protesting a legitimate, democratic U.S. Army training base, and face arrest and six months in jail if we come closer. The question of what makes something legitimate and democratic is a crucial one as our civilization continues its imperial route. As Christians, we must take this question seriously, as legitimacy stems from allegiance, and our allegiance to God risks being captured and subdued by our governments.

Our group of pilgrims from the Student Christian Movement of Canada has traveled to this massive demonstration for three days, each of us bearing a cross with the name of a martyr killed by U.S.-trained officers. We have discussed our own role in upholding and supporting the systems of oppression that make martyrs out of those blessed by Jesus in his Beatitudes; the poor, those who hunger for justice, the peacemakers.

I distinctly remember becoming overwhelmed at the Fort Benning vigil by a sense of the sheer scale of suffering unleashed by our culture in only a few hundred years: the colonization and genocide of Indigenous peoples; the kidnapping and enslavement of Africans; the marginalization of women, the poor, immigrants, and those who identify as LGBTQ today. And what of the earth, torn to shreds by our drive for economic growth and greed?

As the chopper blades thud closer, the military police blast once more the warning of prosecution for our peaceful dissent at the gates of one of the most notorious terrorist training camps in the world. I realize I've been pulled out of my everyday apathy (from *a-pathos*, "not feeling") and have become completely submerged in the suffering and oppression of the poor. And yet, in this timeless space, I feel full of grace and God's presence. We are all in this together, and we are honoring the memories of the martyrs with a celebration of our common humanity and solidarity across borders.

But I can't handle the cacophony any more. No chopper or police warning will shake me from this conviction: love *must* overcome evil, and our love as Christians must be subversive, radical, and risky for it to transform our culture of domination and death. "Radical" literally means getting to the roots; in the words of the young prophet Jeremiah, God has called for us to tear down and to plant (Jeremiah 31:28).

Our love must be subversive

Our vigil group begins to pray, out of a sense that we must turn away from the warnings and numbing threats of incarceration. Instead, we ground ourselves in our mission and faith, through the words that Jesus taught: *Our Father, who art in heaven...*Soon, several nuns join us...*Hallowed be thy name. Thy kingdom come, thy will be done, on earth as it is in Heaven...*Our hands join into a circle, and soon the oppressive racket seems less terrifying, less demoralizing. *Give us this day our daily bread, and forgive us our sins...*Are we not all in need of forgiveness, and in turn try to forgive the oppressors even as we stand in the way of their massacres and torture?...*As we forgive those who sin against us.* I am saved from the temptation to walk away from the gates, to go back to the activist merchandise tables, to pray on my own for solace and peace, to step out of this collective death-space and shut my ears to the droning names of the disappeared, to go back to the busy-ness of taking pictures and interviewing people. *Save us from the time of trial, and deliver us from evil...*

Grace is real. Redemption is possible. God's kingdom, power, and glory are here among us.

On Earth as It Is in Heaven

This essay is about radicalism, and more personally why I am a Christian anarchist.

Before I became a follower of Jesus, I cut my teeth as a spiritual activist in Quebec City in 2001, at demonstrations against the Free Trade Area of the Americas (FTAA). There 60,000 protesters converged on the historic fortified city as thirty-four leaders from across the Western Hemisphere signed a free trade agreement granting massive rights to multinational corporations at the expense of health, environment, and human rights. All of this happened behind closed doors, literally behind a fence and thousands of riot police.

I spent six days on the streets, amid tens of thousands of tear gas canisters, water cannons, and nonviolent protesters arrested and pepper-sprayed. I had been reading Gandhi, had just traveled to his home state in India, and met uneducated people there who could recite the acronyms of global financial institutions like the International Monetary Fund and World Trade Organization because they affected their lives. I realized my ignorance despite my college education.

Inspired by Gandhi, I decided to fast for spiritual purity and nonviolence. At the fence, I witnessed violence meted out coldly by lines of black-clad, masked riot police. Dozens of white streams of gas billowed forth after being shot over the fence; it burned my eyes, mouth, and nose, clung to my clothes, but I stood my ground in tears. A young man approached, holding up a sign, and an officer strode forward calmly, leveled his CS (Counter-Strike) launcher through the fence hole at the man's face, and fired point blank. I will only say that I was glad to be fasting for nonviolence because for a time my hatred burned stronger than the tear gas.

That week I met a gentle leader named Kimi Pernia Domico, whose Embera Katio nation was trying to stop the flooding of his people's land in Colombia, in opposition to the Canadian government's foreign investments and free trade agreement. He questioned why this trade deal (which he called a "corporate bill of rights") should shock us, since for his people it is seen as only the latest step in the theft of indigenous resources by Europeans that started 500 years ago. I could not even imagine a frame of reference beyond my lifetime, let alone across centuries of history.

History and hope overcome Empire

A long-term sense of history and hope is precisely what we need today to overcome Empire. I am not an individual isolated in my choices. Wearing sweatshop-free shoes may be ethical, but it does not stop global violence, nor redress injustice. That is our collective responsibility, and it is one we share with centuries—even millennia—of saints who came before us and, I believe, watch over us today. In my faith, the Communion of Saints has become a meaningful representation of the continuity of history, of people's struggle, and of a deep solidarity that offers support, strength, courage, and consolation in times of disappointment and hopelessness.

Shortly after returning to Colombia after the Quebec protests, Kimi was kidnapped and has never been found. Given the Colombian paramilitaries' links to U.S. military aid (in weapons, cash, and School of the Americas training), it is not inconceivable that his prophetic witness to us in the Global North led to his martyrdom back home.

Though I had been keenly fascinated by meditation and world religions since I was an atheist teenager, I trace my real faith journey to the week I spent in Quebec City, being humbled and awakened. It was there that I met my first saints, in that throng of strangers helping wash tear gas and pepper spray from each other's eyes. They were mentors who would guide and inspire me to prayer, action, ritual, and community.

The saints who guide my life today include Dorothy Day, the Christian anarchist who founded houses of radical hospitality in the Catholic Worker movement; Martin Luther King Jr., whom I honor not only for his vision of beloved community, but for his turning to admonish the sins of imperialism and capitalism later in his life; Sts. Francis and Clare, lovers of simplicity and solidarity; Archbishop Oscar Romero, killed by SOA-graduated killers because he defended the poor.

No saint is perfect, which is a great lesson to us who are obviously imperfect. But they seek to dream and create something better around us. Dorothy Day was, like me, not religious when she was politicized. In Depression era New York City, she was at home with communists, militant unionists, and drunken philosophers until the birth of her child, Tamar. It was the in-breaking presence of this love of her life, and seeing the masses of the poor crowding into the masses of the Catholic Church, which led her to faith.

Day's true radicalism began as a Christian because she was able to attend to the smallest act of loving service—acts such as washing a homeless person's feet, welcoming a refugee, growing her own food. At the same time, she defied war, preaching revolution and decrying the racism and abuse at the heart of her nation.

Like many followers of Christ, Day faced times of trial, literally, under judge and jail-cell, and metaphorically in her struggle to balance nonviolent revolutionary aims and the needs of her family and community. She faced, throughout her life, a "long loneliness;"[1] an alienation and absence that stitched together personal and political issues and drew her toward God. She discovered that such alienation could only be healed in community.

Give Us Today Our Daily Bread and Forgive Us...

Today I work in the Canadian branch of a global network of Student Christian Movements (SCMs), who work toward Christian unity through ecumenism and social justice activism. Though not explicitly an anarchist movement, our mission and our work embody the principles of egalitarianism, inclusiveness, mutual empowerment, and solidarity in a way that has transformed and inspired my faith and politics.

When I think of the handful of courageous people who deliberately trespass onto Fort Benning every year to draw public attention to the blood on our hands, with our tax dollars, I am certain that breaking the law is not the worst sin available to us today. Sin separates us from God; speaking out for the oppressed draws us closer to our neighbor and therefore to our Lord.

Jesus resisted

Jesus routinely broke the laws of his day. He cleared the temple of merchants who made God available only to those who could afford the merchandise and jump through the hoops. He healed the sick on the Sabbath, decreed by law as a day of rest, insisting that love and healing came before religious purity and righteous legalism. Our Lord ate with drunks, sex workers, lepers, and other untouchables. I am convinced that today he would certainly do the same with illegal aliens, queer and transgender people, freedom fighters, Muslims, and those we have discarded and enslaved in our prison industrial complex.

What was unique about Jesus' tactics of resistance to the occupation of his country by the Romans and their client-dictators was that he did not demonize the enemy, though he did severely admonish the religious bigots and imperialists. Nor did he exhort violence. I believe he recognized that revolution without redemption merely risks replacing one dominant group with another.

We know, however, that God is biased in favor of the poor, the widow, and the migrant; this much is clear in the Prophets and Psalms of the Hebrew Scriptures. And we know that God acts in human history and society. God acts directly and through the prophets. God acts to right wrongs, empower the silenced, liberate the oppressed, and lift up the cause of freedom and justice.

This insight about God's "preferential option for the poor" arose from poor Christian communities of Latin America, who inspired the liberation theology movement, which turned every Christian concept on its head. Liberation theology, in many forms around the world today, distinguishes between Christendom-the merged power of the imperial Church and the State-and the body of Christ, which is the whole people of God, crucified in the poor and marginalized. As one of the movement's proponents writes:

> To be followers of Jesus requires that [we] walk with and be committed to the poor; when [we] do, [we] experience an encounter with the Lord who is simultaneously revealed and hidden in the faces of the poor.[2]

I am a Christian anarchist because I take Jesus' call to risky and subversive discipleship very seriously. This necessarily places me into struggle within myself to face my privilege, and into conflict with the powers of domination that govern our world and maintain human control over others.

Out of this sense of struggle I went to Lebanon in 2005, sent by my church to accompany, to learn, and to serve. After months of hearing peoples' stories of exile, human rights abuse, and poverty in Palestinian refugee camps, I witnessed Israel's 2006 military invasion firsthand, and could no longer lie to myself about the reality and depth of our sin.

I have been forced to confront the fact that I no longer believe in progress or voluntary positive change in our society. I even struggle with whether Jesus was a pacifist. When I think in terms of human history, the advances we have supposedly made pale in comparison to the gross power we wield today to destroy all life; to imprison, execute and starve millions; and to deny our oppression beneath the grand illusions of democracy and peace.

However, cultivating mindfulness of beauty, especially in painful times, opens us to the daily bread that can keep us alive. Communion reminds us that God blesses us with what we need to survive (bread) and to thrive (wine) in a broken world.

Globally, our economic system is rooted in centuries of Empire (a political, cultural, and economic system of domination perpetually expanding and exploiting), and it follows millennia of hierarchical violence based on gender, wealth, and the exploitation of the land. In Canada today, we still send in the army when indigenous people question environmental destruction of their lands. Jesus' word for sin (at least in the Lord's Prayer) was closer in meaning to "debt," and today our culture is absolutely dependent on debt and wage slavery (being forced to produce wealth for the elite at the workers' expense).

Idolatry is anything we do that puts our own priorities, or anything else, before God. Anything that demands allegiance of our minds and hearts is an idol demanding sacrifice and worship, blinding us to oppression. I would argue that the system(s) of patriarchal, white supremacist capitalism, in its insatiable consumption, reckless waste, and extremes of wealth and poverty, is idolatry.

It is time to stop thinking of sin as being about our individual choices. Personal responsibility is an important but incomplete aspect of the huge sins that surround and possess us every day. We are all sinners; we are all in debt in some form. Our debt is spiritual, economic, political, historical, and deeply personal all at once. We can make sense of sin in community.

I believe this is the basis for ending oppression. I believe that I am at once part of the problem of injustice, and yet part of systems and histories bigger than I can even imagine. I am white (Irish-Scottish-British), male, and from a wealthy background, born with privilege into the heart of Empire's North American power-center; but at the same time, I identify as gender-queer (I resist this culture's assumptions of what a "man" is and should be) and I live in the inner city. Identity is complex and context-dependent, but we cannot do justice without seeing how oppressions are linked:

racism, sexism, homophobia, imperialism, ageism, ableism, and classism to name but a few. And buttressing all of these systems is an economic system and cultural fabric that we must bring down if we are to liberate ourselves and nurture God's reign breaking into history.

Another word for this path of community, trust, courage, and faith is "discipleship." Discipleship is the practice of following Christ and living out our faith. Some activists, such as Ched Myers, adopt the term "radical discipleship" to deepen this definition in light of political realities. This path is costly and oftentimes painful, but it can also reveal beauty and mystery all around us on life's path. It embodies both the cross (suffering) and the resurrection (liberation from suffering).

As groundbreaking feminist theologian Rosemary Ruether writes in *Liberation Theology*:

> To teach [us] to live humanly, repentantly and yet joyfully…is the task of a Christian theology of revolution… Like the people of the Exodus, we must learn to live by faith [rejoicing] in God's daily grace in the name of those future kingdoms which are not yet here.[3]

Save Us from the Time of Trial and Deliver Us…

> We don't cross borders. The borders crossed us.

I've been thinking about borders for a while now. But it wasn't until my first trip down to the School of the Americas vigil that I truly made the link between the problems in the world and the borders and laws we have created. We crossed the border into the U.S., over the bridge into Detroit, and we cannot speak a word, crushed by the feeling that the border zone is more powerful than a simple arbitrary line between states. I feel chills, deep within. On a good day, my white skin gets me across without hassle. A few years ago I met a Native elder who cannot cross between the U.S. and Canada, within his nation's territory; "Our people don't cross borders," he said. "The borders crossed us."

Having arrived in Georgia, we took part in the die-in at the gates. I stared into the watery eyes of Theresa, fake blood smearing her face, as she took on the death of a Salvadorian housekeeper martyred in 1989. The sheer gravity of this death-space sunk in. A nearby child asked, "Grandpa, is she really dead?" Theresa's limp body erupted in a sob that lasted for minutes. I held her and cried.

This is not a protest, I realized; this is sacred liturgy – a work of the people. We are actors on a stage so much larger than ourselves, a drama that stretches back hundreds of years, but we are not powerless. Our tears, rage, and sense of loss reveal an underlying connection—to each other, to the dead and disappeared, and to all the earth.

Grace is real. Redemption is possible. God's kingdom, power, and glory are here among us, *now and forever. Amen.*

Questions \ for Discussion and Contemplation

1 David Ball considers himself a Christian anarchist because he takes "Jesus' call to risky and subversive discipleship very seriously." Is anarchism the only way to take this call seriously? Would you describe Jesus' call in the same way?

2 What circumstances should cause a person of faith to resist a government policy or action?

3 What should an individual do when his or her religious/spiritual values go against the law? How, if at all, should a faith community supports its congregants in acting in a way that breaks laws?

Kharma R. Amos

5

Too Political for My [Clerical] Shirt

I stood outside the White House waiting to be arrested.

Hundreds of us were there—people of faith engaging in an act of nonviolent civil disobedience in opposition to the war in Iraq. I had no idea in those moments that a jury of my church peers would provide a bigger tussle than civil authorities.

Back at church, certain members of my congregation weren't pleased with my activity. It came as a genuine surprise to me when a few individuals complained that by participating in this protest I was being "too political." The war was not "our issue," they charged.

I was rendered completely speechless.

Such moments are few for me. But I've learned that in the unlikely event I find myself wanting for speech, those moments lead to extremely meaningful spiritual reflection.

Whose Issues, Which Issues?

The congregation I serve is affiliated with Metropolitan Community Churches (MCC), a denomination that was formed forty years ago by gay and lesbian Christians who had been excluded (and, many times, evicted) from other mainline churches because of their sexuality. Still today, a majority of the members of

MCC congregations around the world either identify themselves as lesbian, gay, bisexual, or transgender (LGBT), or they are allies in the struggle for justice in the church and society for LGBT people. We are not a so-called "gay church," but we are a church that celebrates the full inclusion of LGBT families in the beloved community of God.

It's easy to imagine, then, that I've never received complaints when I am a public spokesperson for LGBT equality. I am fully supported each time I write a letter to the editor or lobby a legislator. No one bats an eye when I participate in a community rally that advocates for marriage equality for same-sex couples or work for laws that protect people from discrimination on the basis of actual or perceived sexual orientation or gender identity—not to mention adoption rights for LGBT people or any number of other justice issues related to sexual and gender minorities.

It seems to me that all of these approaches to justice are *highly* political actions.

Yet the White House war protest crossed a line, I was told by congregation members.

As I began to really sit with this quandary, I was reminded of the criticism the Rev. Dr. Martin Luther King Jr. received in response to his public opposition to the war in Vietnam. I remember well the cognitive dissonance I experienced when I first learned that African Americans were among the most vocal critics of King's anti-war speeches. And, to frame that opposition in ways similar to the complaints I received, they did not want him to talk about the war out of fear that doing so would detract from or counteract the progress toward racial equality (i.e., "their issue") being advanced by the civil rights movement. In *The Autobiography of Martin Luther King Jr.*, the great civil rights leader writes:

> Some of my friends of both races and others who do not consider themselves my friends expressed disapproval because I had been voicing concern over the war in Vietnam. In newspaper columns and editorials, both in the Negro and the general press, it was indicated that Martin Luther King Jr. is "getting out of his depth." I was chided, even by fellow civil rights leaders, members of Congress, and brothers of the cloth for "not sticking to the business of civil rights."[1]

This example of people wanting to restrict Dr. King's work for justice solely to matters of race is illustrative of a larger pattern, which I find problematic, in which various minority movements seem to focus their attention only on specific aspects of human experience (e.g., race, gender, sexuality, class, etc.), aspects that are, interestingly, usually also self-descriptive.

The Rev. Nancy Wilson, moderator of MCC, shared with me an experience that further illustrates this false choice between just causes.

In 1977, when the press questioned Rev. Troy Perry, MCC's founder, about MCC's position on a woman's right to choose, he told them the community didn't have a position because it wasn't our issue.

Wilson and other MCC women challenged Perry about this. They aimed to help him understand that lesbians are, in fact, women, and that lesbian identity was complex in that way. They told him that every woman is affected by issues like this one because any woman could be raped. They reminded him that many women who identified as lesbians had previously been heterosexually active, and some of them had had abortions.

Furthermore, everyone, regardless of gender, was personally affected by women's issues, because most have mothers or daughters or other loved ones who may have to face this type of decision. Wilson and others insisted that MCC's commitment to social action—thoroughly rooted in its calling as a community of faith—compelled the church to speak politically about this issue, as well as others.

A New Way to Be Human

I believe a single-issue approach to justice presents several problems. First, it's an approach that is deceptively oversimplified. It fails to explore the complicated ways in which our multilayered identities are constructed. We are never fully described by only our gender, race, ethnicity, sexuality and so on.

Next, it has the effect of setting various justice movements in a posture and a mind-set of competition for a presumably limited amount of rights or freedoms. The 2008 Democratic primary is a good example. Some were conditioned to think that one would *either* achieve an important victory in the struggle for equality for women *or* for people of color—but not both at the same time.

There's another problem. The division of various minority movements into separate and competing categories often further marginalizes the people who exist at the intersections of those categories, or renders them invisible.

Here's an example from the context of LGBT community. Lesbians were historically less than fully considered or included in both the early gay rights movement and the women's movement. The former was sometimes insensitive to the role of sexism and the latter of heterosexism. Likewise, one might note that lesbians and gays of color have not always benefited from the social progresses advanced by various LGBT liberation movements, which were often insensitive to issues of race and class. At the intersection of oppressions, people are marginalized on several accounts. And often they are the ones suffering the effects of injustice the most. *These* are the "least of these" that our faith tells us are on the heart of God and in need of our social and political action.

By trying to define "our issue" neatly and narrowly, framing it as a "civil right" for a particular category of people based on only one aspect of human experience, we miss the broader calling to work for human rights for all people.

*The least of these?
Civil right?
OUR issue?*

It is impossible to lift up only one aspect of our humanity as being more important or definitive than all others. It risks, among other notions, advocacy built on a foundation of arrogance and self-centeredness. I believe we need to make the move from "me, me, me" to "we, we, we" if we are truly to make progress toward establishing justice for all and helping to heal our global community. We have to expand our self-understanding beyond limited notions of race, class, gender, sexuality, or nation and develop an understanding of ourselves as first and foremost human beings.

In *The Preaching Life*, the Rev. Barbara Brown Taylor describes the power of this simple shift in this way:

> Reading the newspaper, I see a map of the world with symbols denoting war, earthquake, famine. There are black lines separating this country from that, this people from

> that. I note with some relief that the area in which I live is free of symbols. I look once and think, "Thank God I'm an American." I look twice and think, "God, help me, I'm an earthling," and in that imaginative act my relationship to the world in which I live is changed.[2]

Following the biblical command to "do justice" can never really be about "just us." I long for the day when we will consider "our issue" any issue that is characterized by injustice and in which personal, cultural, structural, and systemic forces grant privileges to some while oppressing others. Humanity is inherently interdependent. We need to remember this and why it matters.

Unfortunately I think we often conceive of what is "ours" only when we are able to see or feel some personal connection.

For example, many people only learn to care about LGBT equality once they know someone gay who comes out to them. Many white people only learn to deconstruct white privilege and challenge racism when they know someone of a different race and are able to connect with their experience. In some ways, we come to understand that something is ours after we develop or discover a personal investment in it. This made it necessary for me to challenge my church community.

Building on that conversation, we were also able to talk about why other political issues—combating poverty or abolishing capital punishment, for example—are related to "our issue" of working for justice in relation to sexuality. For example:

- What does war have to do with sexuality? One of the oldest strategies of militarism includes the humiliation of enemies through sexual exploitation, including the anal rape of enemy soldiers by presumed heterosexual men. The rape of women and children in "foreign" territories is a constant tactic employed when richer, more powerful countries colonize them, primarily through military campaigns. Additionally, in the United States, many LGBT young adults turn to the military as a way of escaping from homophobic or abusive home situations, even though the government still discriminates against gay and lesbian members of the military based on their sexuality (i.e. "Don't ask, don't tell"). The same institution willing to allow them to serve and die in a time of war will not acknowledge and affirm their right to exist or love the people they love. Justice issues that relate to sexuality are integral components of opposing war and promoting peace.

- What's poverty got to do with sexuality? Poor people around the world are often forced into sex work as the only viable means of making a living. People who cannot afford birth control or abortion are more likely to get pregnant and have children they cannot adequately support, the costs of which further impoverish them. People with inadequate means of procuring protection for safe sex are at a higher risk of infection from sexually transmitted infections and diseases. People without adequate housing, including refugees and children, are unable to protect the integrity of their own bodies and live in a constant state of heightened risk for rape and sexual abuse. Justice issues related to sexuality are integral components of combating poverty.
- What's capital punishment got to do with sexuality? In many parts of the world laws are on the books that criminalize same-sex sexual behavior, or the sexual activity of women outside of state-institutionalized marriage systems. The execution of two young gay men in Iran in 2005 for homosexual conduct is just one example catalogued by groups like Human Rights Watch.[3] The same group reports that women and men continue to be stoned to death for adultery, fornication, and other sexual "violations" in Iran, Nigeria, and several other countries. When we think about people being murdered by the state as criminals for being LGBT, we can begin to notice the inherent injustice of capital punishment, which we might not have noticed when we didn't have a personal connection. Justice issues related to sexuality are integral components of abolishing the death penalty.

When we are attentive to the intersection of oppressions and the complicated nature of individual identity, we are given an opportunity to broaden our perspective and realize that the divisions we make between categories of people and between what constitutes "our issue" and what doesn't are arbitrary at best. I wish it didn't require some form of personal connection to motivate us to care about issues of injustice others are facing. Yet I want us to do whatever it takes for us to understand that any issues related to securing human rights and liberation for all people are "our issues".

Civil or human rights?

I am convinced we must move beyond the goal of individual *civil* rights, by which we gain access to certain rights and privileges for ourselves (generally at the expense of others), toward a goal of establishing *human* rights for every person, rights based solely on their status as a human being rather than some characteristic deemed meritorious or superior by existing systems of privilege.

Too Political? Rubbish!

Helpful dialogue evolved as I exchanged ideas with my congregation. One thing was still a thorn in my side—that "too political" complaint.

Let me say this as plainly as I know how: It is never "too political" for people of faith, including spiritual leaders, to engage in concrete and compassionate acts of service, speech, and/or civil disobedience in order to work for justice. This is, I believe, what God requires of us.

Jesus challenged publicly the institutional entities of his day to hold them accountable for their responsibility to care for all people, especially the poor and marginalized. In this, he stood in a long line of prophets from his faith tradition that did exactly the same thing, criticized both spiritual and political leaders for exploiting the powerless to secure their own privilege and feed their own greed. Throughout the ages, people who were motivated by the core values and deepest convictions of their faith have spoken truth to political power when politicians and political systems were not using that power to promote justice for all. This is the very nature of what it means to put our faith in action as doers of justice.

When I have heard people complain that I am too political as a preacher or spiritual activist, I often think the unspoken message goes something like this: "I just want to hear about love and peace, sweetness and light. Your job is to make me feel good. Don't make me acknowledge the ugliness and pain in the world because it's too hard to face and I feel powerless to do anything about it."

I get that. It is difficult to look honestly at the places of brokenness and despair in our world. It can be overwhelming.

Yet this is precisely where our faith enters in as a resource because we—Christians—are a people of hope.

In the face of humiliation, suffering, and even death, we have a resurrection faith that claims this is not the final word. I believe in a God who is still very much alive in the world. God is painfully aware of the needs of the outcasts and the lowly and still inspiring us to be co-laborers in bringing about a more just and equitable world and way of living together, in the spirit of a poem widely attributed to Saint Teresa of Avila:

> Christ has no body now on earth but yours,
> no hands but yours,
> no feet but yours.
> Yours are the eyes through which the compassion of Christ
>   looks out upon the world,
> yours are the feet by which Christ goes about doing good,
> yours are the hands with which Christ blesses the people.

In order to take that responsibility seriously, we need to be engaged in the world around us and we need to be willing to speak up and act up for justice, both far and near. It's not too political to do so, rather it's not political enough not to do so.

In the Slammer

My night in jail after being arrested outside the White House was deeply, spiritually meaningful for me.

I don't think we talk often enough about the idea that not only does our faith inspire our action, but our political actions can provide opportunities for spiritual growth. As I gathered with more than 3,000 Christians from all over the nation for a long, cold night in Washington, and as I stood in solidarity with those who were arrested, I met some amazing people in whom I saw the face and encountered the heart of Christ.

There was the woman I was paired up with as we marched two by two to the sidewalk in front of the White House. She was a retired P.E. teacher from New York who felt compelled to do something more than talk about peace. Three soldiers from her small town of 8,000 people had been killed. All of them were young men of color. This was her second arrest for civil disobedience.

And there was the woman from Nebraska who said it was her first time to be involved in a protest like this one. She had traveled alone to Washington to participate.

There was also the woman I spent several hours next to on the bus that served as our mobile jail. She was a grandmother of four from Richmond who said this might have been the most important thing she had ever done in her life.

I remember the husband and wife from Knoxville, Tennessee, who had taken one of the older and ill members of the protest group under their wing. He was a stranger to them, but since he was alone and needed extra care, they made sure he got to the front of the line to minimize his time in the cold.

And thanks be to God for the man who circulated through the group distributing Ritz crackers to the hungry, in what I can only describe as one of the most meaningful experiences of Holy Communion I have ever had. In all, 222 people peacefully extended their wrists for cuffing, and in so doing silently followed the example of Jesus, who said, "This is my body!"

These were people who understood that whoever we were and whatever the particulars of our lives, we must learn to come together. We were people of every race, age, sexual orientation, gender identity, economic class, and ability who were called together for action because we couldn't sit by and remain complicit while an unjust war was being waged in Iraq.

As fellow human beings, this was *our issue*, and it required spirit-inspired political action. Today I feel a positive wave of nostalgia wash over me whenever someone complains that I've been "too political," because I remember how humbled I was by the courage of these people and how honored I was to stand with them as an openly lesbian pastor who cares deeply about God's justice and peace.

Questions \ for Discussion and Contemplation

1 Are there any causes that would make you willing to face arrest? What are they? Why?

2 Kharma Amos argues that there are connections between sexuality and other political issues. Do you agree? Why or why not?

3 Can churches become "too political?" How?

wtf?

SECTION TWO

God in the Voting Booth

John Edgerton
Vince Amlin

6

The Ballot Is the Bullet

Voting and Christian Nonviolence

John's Story

The weather could not have been better. November in Chicago can be cold and nasty. But on the night of November 4, 2008, the air was warm and mild. The crowd at Grant Park was tightly packed, but the mood was jubilant as we awaited the election results. Many had brought pocket radios, and news crackled through the crowd like electricity. New York, Massachusetts, New Jersey, Florida, Obama had taken them all. For over five hours I waited in a crowd of seventy thousand people standing shoulder to shoulder. Everywhere around me I could see people shifting uncomfortably, trying to rest tired legs and stretch aching backs.

As the time when the polls would close in California approached, the excitement returned. In a booming collective voice the crowd counted down the seconds, completely focused on the jumbo-sized screen that would announce the results. As the count reached zero, there was a pregnant pause, as if everyone was holding their breath at once. Then, like a giant wave smashing against a cliff, the park exploded into cheers as Barack Obama was declared the winner. I could barely see ten feet in front of my nose. All around me, people were throwing their arms in the air, jumping up and down, and screaming with joy. Jostled from every direction and embraced by total strangers, I could not help feeling isolated and alone. Amid all that excitement, I was an outsider—I had not voted.

This was the election of elections, certainly the biggest in my lifetime and perhaps in many lifetimes. This was the election in which many people invested their deepest hopes, and I sat it out. Intentionally. In fact, I plan to sit out every election for the rest of my life. Why? I am a Christian nonvoter, and I believe that the life and teachings of Christ make abstaining from voting a prophetic witness to American society. I am committed to pacifism and nonviolent social action. Jesus Christ teaches that we must love our enemies and that when others threaten or harm us, we must turn the other cheek. This is not an easy command, but Christ's own constant refusal to use violence—even in the face of his own death—tells me that if I want to follow Jesus, I must give up violence in all forms. And voting is violent.

Violence and Voting

Voting is violent?

Most of us think about voting for a President as choosing between candidates, deciding who is best suited for the position. This is only part of the story. We are also voting to place someone in the office of President. This office, like any, comes with a job description, part of which is the role of Commander in Chief of the armed forces. When we vote, we collectively decide to give one person control over the deadliest weapon in the world, the U.S. military, and authorize him or her to use it whenever necessary. Voting in a Presidential election does more than simply express a preference. Voting also affirms the broader political order of our nation, and that political order is not peaceful.

As I considered the possible results of 2008's election, I realized with great sadness that no matter who won, our nation would not love its enemies and would most certainly not turn the other cheek. Instead, our military spending will remain unprecedented, and we will continue to export weaponry across the world. Most disturbingly, our nation will maintain its stockpile of nuclear weapons. That arsenal is so large and destructive it could kill every one of Earth's six and a half billion people several times over and make creation unfit for life for tens of thousands of years. These mechanisms of death-dealing are our nation's form of security.

Our nation trusts in violence to keep us from violence. We trust in annihilation for our protection.

Perhaps as a reader you are thinking at this point that if I want to change the country, then I should vote. But the process of voting itself feeds our nation's violence because it breeds anger and operates through fear and division. The Presidential election of 2008 provided plenty of evidence for this. Many were horrified when they read about the school bus filled with elementary-aged children in Madison County, Idaho, chanting "Assassinate Obama!" Earlier in the election season an effigy of Republican Vice Presidential candidate Sarah Palin was hung by a noose outside a West Hollywood home. These examples draw on the power of violence to incite others to action, and they treat murder and lynching as acceptable political expressions.

Of course, most of us haven't hung any effigies or shouted any death threats. But the same kind of poisonous hate is found in more familiar forms. Do you read political blogs, or post comments on a newspaper's online message board, or listen to AM talk radio? Every single day there are thousands of examples of Americans talking about their political enemies in hateful, violent ways: "Someone needs to take Cheney out to the woods and shoot *him*" or "Give me five minutes alone in a windowless room with an abortionist, I'd teach them how real Americans feel about baby killers." We are tempted to use hateful slurs and talk about how much we want to hurt those who disagree with us. This kind of communication is common, clear evidence that our political thinking is poisoned by anger and violence.

Bloggers and pundits, however, are not shock figures preying on our baser impulses. They simply display more clearly than most the angry divisiveness that exemplifies American politics. Even the largest and most reputable media sources depend on such division for ratings and readership. The computer mapping systems of CNN and MSNBC have made us all acutely color conscious. Electoral politics and the media that cover them depend on drawing battle lines between Republicans and Democrats. Red or blue, us or them, that is how we are encouraged to think. Election coverage reads like a war being measured in votes. Early primary contests are often called "skirmishes" before the general election, which will be

Division wins elections.

decided in "battleground states." Our political division is so stark that it seems only natural to use the language of violence and war.

Division is the way elections are won. In our nation's system, trying to win with 100% of the vote would be a disastrous strategy. American politics unabashedly operates by finding and exploiting "wedge issues," those disagreements that can sharply divide voters into two camps. Politicians, pundits, and private individuals drive these wedges deep, creating seemingly irresolvable conflicts between neighbors. The things we count most precious, about which we care most deeply, are exploited for cynical political purposes. They know how to push our buttons, and by November we are whipped into frenzy. That is why elections are so stressful. Campaigns prey on our political divisions in order to make us fearful of other people, fearful of those whom Christ teaches us to love. Every election cycle has its own unique boogieman, that new terrifying problem that each party claims it will fix. Maybe foreign workers will be prolonging the recession. Or maybe terrorists will be plotting mass murder. Or maybe the welfare doles will be eroding our nation's work ethic. All political campaigns promise hope and prosperity in victory and threaten disaster in defeat. Rest assured the next election will be no different. We are a country organized around division and motivated by fear.

It is no surprise, then, that the United States military is more powerful than any other in human history. We cannot find common ground with each other, and we fear that other nations will not find common ground with us. So our nation arms itself to the teeth, maintains military dominance over any other single nation and has a nuclear arsenal continually ready to launch. Voting for a candidate who is marginally less hawkish than another cannot solve the problem of American violence. The system itself breeds division, fear, and violence.

* EVERY human being

As Christians, however, we don't need to live like this. The good news of Jesus Christ is that every human being is a beloved child of God. Each and every person in the world is so valuable that God became a human being and lived as one of us, to teach us how to treat each other. Jesus prays "that they may all be one," (John 17:11, 21 and 22) pleading for an end to all the false divisions that human beings draw—racial, economic, national, political, and sexual. Our sinful fear and anger tell us that these false divisions are important, that by defeating our sisters and brothers we can keep ourselves from danger. As Christians, we know the truth: we are one people in Christ. This divine unity extends to every aspect of our shared lives, including our political decisions.

As Christians, we are called to witness to this unity, to tell this good news to a world that does not know its source or its power. I am not advocating a selfish withdrawal from the world, or false piety that retreats from the terrible problems facing our country and our world. On the contrary, faith in Jesus Christ always strains to reach beyond itself. It seeks to create new bonds of community and heal social wounds. The social action that God calls Christians to engage in cannot be organized around win or lose political decisions. You cannot build a house of prayer for all people with tools made only to divide.

But there are other tools.

Vince's Story

Last summer, while I interned in a Mennonite community in Chicago, I got to experience one of those "other tools" up close. I witnessed a congregation changing the world by replacing the fear, hatred, and division of voting with the trust, peace, and unity of a consensus model of decision making. This community is no ordinary congregation. Its members live together, share salaries in a "common purse," and run social service agencies for children and the elderly. They also buy and manage apartment buildings to increase the amount of low-cost housing available in a rapidly gentrifying neighborhood. When a large building came on the market this summer, some members wondered if God might be calling them to buy it, and I got my first taste of a nonviolent alternative to voting: the consensus process.

The building for sale was made up of studio apartments and had the lowest rents on the block. Such housing is often the last barrier between individuals and homelessness. Church members began to ask one another whether they should buy the building, priced at 3 million dollars, to ensure that it remained affordable. This was a big decision and would have to come before the entire congregation. I started to get nervous: I have seen congregations pulled apart by questions of how to handle property and have witnessed people storming out of sanctuaries over much smaller sums.

I walked into the first meeting feeling both excited and apprehensive. How would this close-knit, peaceful congregation tackle such a difficult decision? After a time of prayer and singing, one of the people who felt called to buy the building came forward to explain his reasoning. He spoke matter-of-factly about the blessings and challenges of doing so. He explained that the church didn't have anything like 3 million dollars to buy the building outright. Instead, they would have to mortgage the building and raise rents on their other low-cost apartments. He closed by saying that they would need to bid within the month, and unless the entire community agreed by their next monthly meeting, they would not buy the building. I was shocked by how honest his description was. If he was trying to convince those who would be opposed, his strategy seemed odd to say the least.

As he sat down, others were invited to express their thoughts about the purchase. I braced myself for a screaming match, but instead person after person calmly offered their ideas. The sentiments were heartfelt, and the questions were probing, but no one spoke angrily or accusingly. After an hour the meeting wound down with the announcement that there would be three more meetings to discuss the matter and that someone had brought cobbler.

At the following meetings, conversation about the proposal grew deeper and more detailed. I listened to members contribute, all the while separating them into two camps—"for" and "against." I was thinking about it like an election. I imagined alliances forming and secret conversations taking place during our post-meeting desserts. To my eyes, those "against" seemed far from persuaded. Every meeting, they brought forward more considered objections. Far from moving toward consensus, each meeting gave me the feeling that the group would never unanimously agree.

After four weeks, the time had come. I was sure that the pressure of arriving at a decision would finally lead to the flaring tempers I had envisioned all along. I waited for the drama of election night, for last-second mudslinging, or an "October surprise." After a scripture reading and a few hymns, the man who had spoken first a month ago came forward to tell the group again why he believed the church should buy the building. I hoped for a lawyer's masterful closing argument, but he spoke in much the same way he had at every other meeting. He acknowledged the serious objections that had been raised over the last month. There would be many challenges, he agreed, but he still believed that God was calling the community to help the poor by buying the apartment building.

He sat down, and the meeting continued. Those who had been opposed to the project still had their reservations and restated their opinions. It seemed clear to me that the meeting would never result in consensus. One woman who had been silent so far stood up to speak. "I'm just exhausted. I've got so much going on right now. I can't possibly take on another thing." My heart sank, I thought the ugly conflict I had feared was about to explode. She continued, "I just don't have the energy to take on this building, but if others feel called to do it, I won't stand in their way. My tiredness is no reason to oppose the Spirit. I think we should go ahead." The meeting continued with folks speaking both "for" and "against." So I was surprised when, after an hour, the meeting organizer stood up and said: "I sense we might have consensus. Plus, I believe someone has brought ice cream and fresh strawberries, so could we just see hands? Those for? Any opposed? No? It looks like we're going to be buying a new building."

I was floored. I thought that the community had been split down the middle. Hadn't there been people who disagreed even to the end? Someone suggested that we pray over the building we had just decided to purchase. We left the church and filed down the street singing an African hymn:

"Somandela Iesu."
"We will follow.
We will follow Jesus.
We will follow everywhere He goes."

As the song ended, we joined hands in front of the building and bowed our heads. We gave thanks to God for leading us to this decision. We asked God to bless the building and its inhabitants, and to lead us in our continued work in the neighborhood. I walked back stunned, confused about what I had experienced. What did I miss?

In the weeks after that night, I tried to reconstruct what had gone on in that month of meetings. The tired woman's comment stuck with me, her willingness to say "yes" despite her own misgivings. I gradually realized that I hadn't even understood the question being discussed at those meetings. I had believed we were debating whether to buy the building, but the community had been answering the question, "Where is God calling us?" Expecting division, my question had separated the group into "for" and "against." Their question had united them in seeking the will of God. Expecting fear, I waited for someone to say, "If we do this, we could lose our homes, our church. We could be ruined." No one did. Instead, they trusted that those who heard the call of God were listening faithfully. If so, how could they refuse? Expecting violence, I waited for a fight. Instead, we sang a hymn, said a prayer, and ate together.

As that community knows, and as I have begun to learn, we who follow Christ have antidotes for division, fear, and violence. We have been given the antidote to division in the unity of Christ's body. This unity, which we have sorely tested, is real. It is the unity of asking a different question—not "What do I want?" or "What do I need?" or even "What is best?" but "What does God want?" It is the unity of the Lord's Prayer, in which we ask for God's will to be done. We have been given the antidote to fear in the assurance that God is real, and God is good. We are free to take the advice of Christ, who bids us not to be anxious, but to consider the grass of the fields and the birds of the air and to know God's loving care. We no longer need to fear that one party or the other might take control, for our mission remains the same: to be the Church, no matter the cost or the consequences, to follow Jesus everywhere he goes. We have been given the antidote to violence in the peace of Christ that we exchange each week. This peace seeks reconciliation above cessation of conflict. It calls us not to place the least hawkish candidate into the position of Commander in Chief but to work for the dissolution of any office built on violence, for the elimination of all weapons, and for love and understanding between all people.

We have the antidotes, and we are called to share them. We are called to witness to our truth by living lives of contrast, to be salt and light. That is why I do not vote. I do not vote because I have traveled on two different roads. One way divides the world into "us" and "them," the other believes that we are one body with many members. One way depends on the fear of death and destruction, the other relies on trust in neighbor and faith in God. One way sanctions the violence of war and the deterrence of force. It breeds anger and hostility, not only between nations but also between individuals. The other way is leading me to let go of violence so that I can witness to others about the freedom found in love. I do not vote because God has called me to walk that other road, and I am trying to follow.

Questions for Discussion and Contemplation

1 Do you think there is something violent about voting? about democracy? Why or why not?

2 What do you think of the "consensus" model for decision making? What makes it work? Is it more just than voting?

3 Is violence ever justified? When? What makes it justifiable?

wtf?

Kat Banakis

Politeuomai

It was at the Western Wall in the Old City of Jerusalem that I learned politics and religion are co-conspirators toward the mission of loving neighbors well.

To get to the Western Wall you have to weave through a labyrinth of narrow cobblestone streets. The bright desert sun is blocked by a mixture of awnings, airborne grease (from what look like Jamaican kettle drums frying falafel balls) and frankincense burning to show tourists how to do it if they buy some, just a little.

So cheap, so cheap. And 100% real, like the gift for Jesus.

Depending on which part of the Old City you're in, certain smells take precedence. In the Muslim quarter there is more falafel and more humanity. Children and dogs weave in between tourists' legs, and shrouded women elbow past to go into the dressmaker's shop or to do that day's shopping at the produce market. The Muslims seem to actually live their lives within the Old City.

The Christian section spreads out more or less from the Church of the Holy Sepulchre. It's venerated by many Christians as the symbolic (if not geographic) sight of Golgotha, where Christ was killed and buried. Since the fourth century the church has been a site of pilgrimage and devotion for Christians, though the building itself has changed over time. Today the church boasts a lavish rotunda, vibrant icons, glass cases, and many feet of velvet rope protecting holy objects from curious tourists.

The church is co-run by the Greek Orthodox, Armenian Orthodox, and Roman Catholic churches, all of whom claim a degree of precedence and ownership over the holy site. Each morning the holiest of churches is unlocked by an unassuming-looking Muslim layman using a key on a large metal ring of dozens of keys, like the one my elementary school janitor used to carry. In 1192 all of the Christian factions claiming ownership of the church agreed for the sake of peace that none of them could hold the keys to the church. So much for Christian unity, but I appreciate the pragmatism. The delicate *détente* between Christian factions regularly breaks out into violent fights between various monks with police being called to pull committed Christian religious people off of one another.

The hawker stalls leading away from the church stock Christian memorabilia, mostly appealing to ritualistic forms of Christianity. Holy oil, icons, candles, incense, and prayer beads fill each interchangeable stall. Hawkers entertain bargaining, though it feels a little odd to shake someone down for objects of religious devotion. I got one icon for $8 in Jerusalem! It'd be at least four times that price anywhere in the U.S.

Only inside the Church of the Holy Sepulchre can I even try to identify who is there for religious purposes and who for pure tourism, but the two impulses blur. As I kneel down to pray at one altar carved into a cold grotto in the church, a woman some years older than I descends onto the kneeler next to me, resting her camera on the rail where most people rest their hands or foreheads in prayer. Ignoring the pictograph signs with a red line through cameras on every available wall, she looks straight ahead at the altar as if in prayer while her hands, seemingly with a devotional mind of their own, snap dozens of pictures without the benefit of her eyes looking through the viewfinder. She continues looking straight ahead until her hands are done. Then she nods to the altar, stands up, and leaves.

The Jewish quarter is somewhere between the overt religious tourism of the Christian quarter and the commercial bustle of the Muslim quarter. Many of the Jews in the Old City live in Jerusalem part-time or are there on an extended trip. There seem to be the most restaurants in the Jewish quarter, particularly cafés of the "come-and-stay-a while" variety. Seeking to meet neither the residential needs of the Muslim quarter nor the in-and-out tour bus stop of the Christian quarter, the Jewish quarter caters to people who intend to spend time there and to remember the time spent there once they leave. The souvenirs appear to be of decent quality and worthy of coffee table display; tea sets, tapestries, and other knickknacks that could arguably be functional, even if they are purchased primarily for their forms.

The streets of the Old City, with their ancient stones and women shrouded in scarves and male monks shrouded in cassocks are unfamiliar to me. I'm used to newer roads.

In my years working as a lobbyist for affordable housing and homeless people in Washington D.C. I became accustomed to the roads laid out in wheel-spoke roundabouts and to traveling on the color-coordinated Metro system. K Street NW, the famed thoroughfare in Washington where many lobbyists' offices are located, hums during workweeks when Congress is in session. Cabs and buses honk. People rush on foot. And many seem to talk with people who aren't physically present, whether on the other end of a cell phone or singing to them from an iPod.

I became accustomed to wearing rubber-soled shoes and carrying an extra black umbrella. When my clients came to town the fastest way to get them around Capitol Hill was to walk back and forth, putting in lateral miles while zigzagging between offices on either side of the Capitol. Inevitably it would rain.

I got used to walking while reading from a tiny personal computer screen because when a bill was on the floor of the House or Senate, edits would be sent around via e-mail, and my colleagues and I would have moments to review the legislation to find out whether it would build more or less homeless shelters where our clients were. I learned to tread lightly in friendships because anyone could be an ally or an opponent on a given day, depending on what issue was on the legislative calendar.

Then I left Washington for seminary and learned to walk new cobblestone paths made to look old. I left Washington for seminary not out of disgust for politics and policy but rather because of what I saw as the most effective lobbying. Time and again long-term change was enacted by careful, thoughtful local citizens working diligently with their local senators and representatives to change policy little by little toward their best guess at justice. I thought Jesus had something to say about policy, that what happens each Sunday during worship ought to be creating citizens who live out their politics on the first Tuesday in November and every day in between. But in the transition between the two worlds of politics and faith, I wasn't so sure.

I began to relearn academic jargon and tried to move according to daily prayer offices—morning, mid-morning, and evening. To get to prayers and classes at the divinity school, I gave up my professional-looking shoes for graduate student-appropriate clogs for walking up a hill each day, and I carried a backpack, one impossibly brimming with books. My classmates murmured to themselves along the walkways of the quad, memorizing biblical Greek gerunds and practicing chant tones. Each day's uphill schlep felt…uphill. When I was lobbying and did my job well, it resulted in specific government money set aside for a homeless shelter or a road resurfacing or an after-school program. When I did my job well in seminary I got a decent grade on a paper that only my professor and I ever saw.

A friend guides me through the dark, winding streets of the Old City of Jerusalem with the surefootedness of a mountain goat (or an experienced pickpocket) until we reach a glass security stall through which all must pass to enter the Western Wall area. In Jewish tradition the wall is thought to be a remnant of King David's Temple as well as the Second Temple. It is the holiest of Jewish sites and sometimes called the Wailing Wall. Observant Jews still go there to mourn the Temple destruction. The wall also serves as a holy site for Muslims, who refer to the wall as either "el-Mabka" ("the place of wailing," referring to Jewish attachment to and sometimes ownership of the wall) or "al-Buraq" (based on the tradition that Muhammad tied up his centaur, Buraq, at the wall). A holy site for both Jews and Muslims for centuries, it has been the site of violent geopolitical strife.

For the sake of uniformity in appearance all new construction or reconstruction in the Old City must be covered in the same brown-gold stone as the ancient buildings. From afar the whole city glistens with a Midas touch. Up close though, it's rather odd and Disneyesque to have a state-of-the-art security stall outfitted with cameras, lasers, and air puffers covered with desert rocks, not unlike the new faux downtowns that popped up throughout the United States in the last decade or so.

Cheering and yelling come from the other side of the security stall. Ejected through the air puffer machine and into the Wall arena I stumble into a crowd of bullhorns, noisemakers, and posters that say in English variations on "Congratulations!" "Way to Go!" "Class of 2007!" I assume the Hebrew writing says the same thing. The crowd is held back by Israeli military police outfitted with large weapons, though they seem to be mostly for show since the crowd isn't trying to move at all. To my left a young soldier marches past with intense concentration, one foot in front of the other and weapon held in front with locked elbows. He disappears into a pool of other similarly young, erect soldiers who welcome him with shout of "Hooah"–apparently a transnational military salute. I wonder if the U.S. Army knows that its cheer has been adopted without adaptation and if they care. I turn back to see if my friend has come through security and see a whole parade of young soldiers of both genders coming down the road. An overhead PA system announces names. I am attending the graduation ceremony for entering recruits of the Israeli army, a mandatory service for all Israeli citizens for a two-year period beginning at age eighteen.

My friend and I try to politely elbow our way through the crowd to get to the actual Western Wall. On the other side of the military blockade men and women, many of whom appear to be Orthodox Jews, *daveen* (bow) separately. As we make our way to the women's part of the wall the graduation ceremony behind me grows somewhat quieter, but no specific sound replaces it. The faithful pray in nearly silent murmurs, and shuffle, carefully avoiding other women in devotion. By custom, after praying at the wall one is to depart walking backward, continuing to face the wall. When one of the faithful bumps into another, neither utters excuse or apology. Everyone just continues in their paths of prayer, avoiding eye contact to observe privacy in the midst of a crowd.

In the midst of the holiest of holy places, I realize that it is perfectly fitting to have "hoo-hah" and "amen" uttered in the same air. In this holiest of places, with stones older than any university could ever attempt to seem, stones ground down with the feet of millions of pilgrims, the proverbial road begins to make sense. There has never been a separation between the political and religious. Early Christian Father Tertullian famously questioned the relationship between religion and politics when he wrote, "What has Jerusalem to do with Athens?" In modern American terms, what has Jerusalem to do with Washington? There, in Jerusalem, it occurs to me that Jerusalem has everything to do with Washington. Religion and politics necessarily inform each other because the political is the world in which we live, the world in which God has placed us to live.

Theology of the incarnation tries to describe how humanity itself is changed in Christ so that we are no longer sinners, but are redeemed and made capable of doing God's work in the world because Christ came in human form and thereby showed us what it means to be human. In his book *The Incarnation of the Son of God*, former Archbishop of Canterbury Charles Gore describes Jesus: "As Son of Man He shows us what human nature is to be individually and socially, and supplies us with the motives and the means for making the ideal real."[1] In becoming human Jesus changed what it means to be human and infuses us with the capability and motivation to live out God's ideals of justice and mercy. Our day-to-day lives and relationships then are the canvas against which the story of God's relationship with humanity is played out, and we are cognizant, willful, and capable actors in that story. If the incarnation makes us actors with God in our daily lives, then what we do in our lives matters greatly. Washington matters because of what happened in Jerusalem. It seems only right to have breakfast with the Bible in one hand and the newspaper in the other, as theologian Karl Barth is said to have done.

Jerusalem has everything to do with Washington.

There's a great passage in Philippians where Paul is instructing that early, small Christian community on how to make a go of it in the period between Christ's resurrection and return. Paul writes, "*Politeuomai* in a manner worthy of the gospel of Christ, so that, whether I come and see you or am absent and hear about you, I will know that you are standing firm in one spirit, striving side by side with one mind for the faith of the gospel" (Philippians 1:27). Most biblical translations translate this word as "live," that is to "live out your life in a manner worthy of the gospel," yada yada yada.

But the verb used there comes from political life and would not have been lost on the Philippians. So it's better translated "live as a citizen" or "engage in politics" or "live out your political life" in a manner worthy of the gospel.

OUR POLITICS MATTER!

Our politics matter. The political lives of Christians matter because change is effected through the arena of politics and policy. Because our political lives matter, then political literacy becomes something more than just part of living as a citizen. Political literacy takes on the status of Christian stewardship of our time, talent, and intelligence. Awareness of politics, policy, and how change takes place within those systems is how we as Christians live out our faith.

In the Benedictine monastic tradition the life of the brothers was divided between times of communal prayer and work that was meant to better the world and community *(ora et labora),* with one informing the other. So too is political life part of our work as Christians, and it must inform our prayer and worship just as our prayer and worship must inform our politics. There, standing at the Western wall, the path between Washington and seminary seemed less vertical than horizontal, a long journey where I would always be walking precariously down the middle.

Whether one says that the Church as an institution should or should not be involved in matters of policy and politics is a topic for another essay and countless books of theory. But the question of our call as individual Christians is a matter of the *labora,* the day-to-day work of Christians on Earth. I agree with Phillip Gamwell, author of *Politics as a Christian Vocation,* that it is the call and vocation of Christians to engage politically because it is through public policy that we enact programs that try to ensure justice and mercy in our world. If we are to try, as Jesus commanded, to love our neighbors, then we are called to care for them in tangible ways and try to provide for their well-being. Governmental policies impact the lives of people of faith and their neighbors one way or another. Remaining ignorant about how policy is made in our lives turns our backs on the world in which we have been placed by God to live holy lives as cocreators with that God.

That day Philippians didn't seem so ancient. *Politeuomai* in a manner worthy of the gospel of Christ.

My friend and I finish our prayers and back up all the way to the proud military families. Upright again we turn and walk out through another security gate on the other side of the walled area, similarly coved in gold stones. Tour buses honk and jerk, dumping out dozens of religious tourists, not unlike myself. We make our way up several flights of stairs to a lookout point often used for panoramic photos of the Old City. The rotunda of the Dome of the Rock and the Church of the Holy Sepulchre in the Old City look not unlike the Capitol building in Washington.

I am grateful for the perspective.

Questions \ for Discussion and Contemplation

1 Have you ever "walked different paths" in your life? How has your perspective changed from one path to another? What has influenced the way you look at the world?

2 What are ways that public policy affects your daily life? the lives of your friends and family?

3 Do you think people of faith have a responsibility to be involved in how public policy is made? Does real change happen through policy making? Why or why not?

Steve Holt

8

Liturgical Politics

Bringing Faith to the Streets

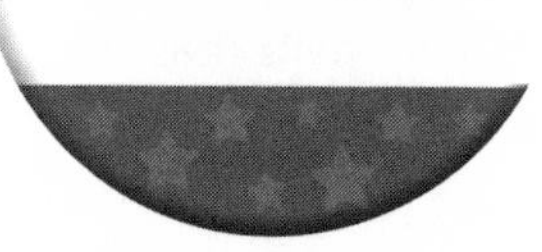

There wasn't a pew or a padded chair to be found. Not a potluck planned or a choir anthem sung. Instead, we hit the streets that day. We created church.

I swung a thurible full of incense among the crowds gathered, just as I would in a large cathedral preparing to celebrate the Mass. But this certainly wasn't a cathedral; rather, it was Century Boulevard, one of the main streets near the Los Angeles International Airport. We had gathered from across Los Angeles to support housekeepers and other workers at five of the airport hotels. Their health and safety had been put at risk by owners trying to get every last cent of profit out of them—giving no overtime, few if any benefits, almost no breaks, and low pay for literally backbreaking work. Almost all of the housekeepers experienced pain through the course of the day; most of them could not even finish their work if not for painkillers. They were working with one of the unions in L.A. to improve their working conditions through a collectively bargained contract, but they were meeting with harsh resistance. Many workers had lost their jobs, others had been threatened and harassed, and no end was in sight.

We came out that night to show these hotel workers we were in solidarity with them. Workers from other unions, students, clergy, members of community organizations, and others were all part of this huge event. We also wanted to let the hotels know that as long as they were not treating their employees with the dignity and respect they deserved, the community would not support their businesses. Management was accountable to the people who lived and worked there and could not expect to get away with treating their workers that way.

We had permits to shut Century Boulevard down between two of the hotels, and we marched, sang, and spoke out for the need for justice for our brothers and sisters.

For me it had already been a long day. I had just started as an intern for Clergy and Laity United for Economic Justice (CLUE). CLUE works with people of all faiths to bring a religious voice to important issues of economic justice across L.A. The main march and rally started at 5 p.m., but much earlier we had been visiting local churches and campuses that were supporting the hotel workers, holding smaller events. By the time we started on Century, I had already walked a few miles, sang and chanted for hours, and even pushed a few wheelchairs for hotel workers in too much pain to do the walking.

In the midst of that rally, though, I could feel new energy rise within me. I reveled in all the people gathered together—of all ages and backgrounds—to sing and chant and speak out for the workers. This was church: an event bringing together people from all walks of life to celebrate and make space for God's transformative work to take place.

I walked one more lap from the Hilton to the Westin, in my cassock and surplice, swinging the censer from side to side.

When we arrived at the Westin Hotel, people preached. We participated in sermons that cried out for justice for the workers. We encouraged them in their struggle. The promise that God was not only concerned with what was happening at those hotels, but also was on the side of the workers who were being oppressed and mistreated, was heard.

Preachers named the specific offenses that had occurred at the hotels, giving the details of why the conditions were immoral. They told stories of those who had been intimidated and harassed for trying to change those conditions. I listened in great anticipation as they told the owners of the hotels that we would not be satisfied with anything short of full repentance, turning away from their current way of doing things, and giving dignity and respect to the housekeepers and other employees.

The event had intentionally been planned around the "Day of the Dead," an important Mexican religious celebration that honors friends and family members who have died. Our event was renamed the "Day of the Dead Tired," bringing attention and honor to those who, because of their working conditions, were exhausted and in pain and distress.

The visual focal point—the ritual object, if you will—was a large quilt, made up of hundreds of 1′ by 1′ squares. Each square represented the story of one of the workers at the hotels, with orange, yellow, and other squares each representing a story of chronic pain, getting fired for organizing, or some other traumatic experience. Most poignant for me was when some of the housekeepers told the stories of the eight black squares, each one the story of someone who had died or had a miscarriage on the job. We shared, lifted up and prayed for all of those whose stories were sewn into the quilt, and I slowly walked around it, using the incense as a powerful aromatic symbol of the prayers that we were bringing for all of these people.

Clergy were not the only ones given the opportunity to speak. All of the many different groups of people who were there had the opportunity to raise their voices. Most important, the housekeepers themselves spoke. One by one they stood up and spoke the truth about what was happening at the hotels, about the pain, the suffering, and the deliberate violations of their rights, as hotel management stood there listening and taking note of the leaders.

When everything else quieted down, the pastors, priests, rabbis, and imams who were part of the event made themselves available for prayer. Long lines formed behind each one as worker after worker received a blessing and prayer for the healing of their pain. This is what we had come together for: mutual support, healing, and ultimately, justice.

My idea of church would never be the same.

That service in October 2007 was a milestone for me to bring together my faith and politics. The journey actually started about six years earlier, one summer in Port-au-Prince, Haiti. I decided to join my church on a ten-day trip. We were invited by a group of local pastors to help run a vacation Bible school for a large group of children and to help with some construction they were doing on the school and church building. I thought it would be a great chance for me to help some people who were in need, but I never would have guessed that I was the one who needed that trip.

I was living in Boston at the time, so arriving in Haiti was a complete shock. Port-au-Prince is one of the poorest cities in the world, and some of its neighborhoods–such as Cité Soleil, where part of our team was working–are home to extreme poverty. The conditions are terrible, but people live in them every single day. These are real people with whom I had the chance to talk, eat, and even worship. Whatever help I could offer them would not compare to how much they were teaching me, as I began to see what real, tested faith actually looked like.

Theirs was a faith that could face the most difficult circumstances, which I had never experienced in the suburbs, and still believe that God was present and acting in the midst of those situations. My heart was broken, but in that process I could see my faith growing and changing to reflect what I had learned from my Haitian brothers and sisters. I also felt myself being called to make a deeper commitment to serving God in places of poverty. So began my call into ministry.

Eventually I discovered that what mattered to me had also mattered to Moses, Isaiah, Amos, Jesus, Paul, and so many of the other prophets. It was a revelation that helped me connect the dots between my faith and the desire to bring healing to the world. That summer, I spent what free time I had rereading the scriptures and finding whatever books I could to help me learn more about God's vision for society.

Having grown up in the Assemblies of God and Evangelical Free churches, whose traditions I appreciated, I was used to their styles of worship. My mother, though, was Roman Catholic, and I also loved the richness of Catholic rituals, particularly the celebration of the Lord's Supper. During that summer, I decided I wanted to integrate all my different Christian experiences: the evangelical, charismatic, and sacramental traditions. As I searched for how to do that, many people directed me toward the Anglican Communion, a historically and liturgically rich tradition that openly embraced a variety of Christian practices.

I immediately felt as if I belonged in that church, and within six months I had been confirmed and was considering the Anglican priesthood.

It was no accident that both of these changes happened at the same time. A deeper understanding of the world I lived in required a deeper understanding of my faith in order to meet the challenges of injustice and overcome them. The spiritual sustenance I was receiving from liturgical practices allowed me to explore more of how my faith affected my vision for society, even when the culture around me seemed hostile toward my new vision.

We frequently come to the political process with misconceptions about what it is, who it serves, and how we participate in it. Is it about choosing a candidate once every four years? Moreover, it often seems it doesn't matter which candidate gets elected, as politics only serve people with money and influence anyway. The only campaign promises apparently acted on are the ones made to major donors, party officials, and close friends. Why waste energy on a process like that?

Working with CLUE has helped me see past that narrow definition of politics. For people of faith, politics is so much deeper than that, and it points to many other opportunities to be engaged besides the voting booth. Every faith tradition teaches that from God's point of view a society is measured by the way it treats its poorest and weakest members: the people most likely to be kept out of the halls of power and forced to fend for themselves.

The laws of the Hebrew Scriptures are especially concerned with protecting people such as the hired laborer, the widow, the orphan, and the immigrant. Christ then announced at the outset of his ministry that he had been anointed to preach good news to the poor.

When the prophets saw that this was not happening in Israel, they did not vote. They marched into the halls of power and spoke directly to the kings and their courts about the injustices and problems of the nation. In an age where our politicians and leaders can be reached through a letter, a phone call, or an e-mail, it is easy to see how we can engage the political process likewise.

But that is not where they stopped. When directly addressing the people with power did not work, they took their message to the community to speak out about necessary changes. They spoke out, not only with words, but also with dramatic presentations that brought the stories to life.

That is where our liturgies can come in.

Liturgy is another term surrounded by misconceptions. When many people hear the word *liturgy,* they think of a rigid set of rules used by a faith community in its own worship services. It is often perceived as confined to a church or other house of worship, having little contemporary meaning. Liturgy in this context is, for the most part, outdated and irrelevant.

Liturgies are more than that, however. They are the shared stories of our faith traditions that not only can reach back into the history of where we have been but also can shape who we are now and direct us toward the future we desire. They have the power to span the entire history and geography of our faiths, while continuing to propel them forward into new times and places. The liturgies of our faith traditions are powerful because they unite us in community; they root us in tradition; they engage all of who we are and where we are; they point us toward something greater than ourselves.

When my church celebrates Christ in the Eucharist on Sundays—our principal liturgical service—I receive the spiritual strength that I need for the week. That Eucharistic liturgy is the shared story of the Christian faith, going back two thousand years and all across the world to offer meaning in my church, in its own time and place.

However, these liturgies were never meant to be locked up and contained in the buildings we call churches and used for the purposes of a small, insulated group of people. Liturgy, in its truest and purest form, engages a broken world and transforms it. During the worship service, everyone is invited to participate and come to the table as equal partners; there is no place for distinctions of class, age, sex, race, or any other kind. We become focused on God, and the place for each of us is as one of God's children. Consequently we experience a different reality that provides a vision of what our world could be, and we are empowered to bring about that vision.

Liturgy engages a broken world and transforms it.

When we held our service on Century Boulevard, the hotel owners gave us no signs that they would change their practices toward their workers. As people of faith, we came out that day to bring the hope that we had experienced in our own sacred services to Century Boulevard. We believed that the hope found in our liturgical practices could lift up the hearts of the employees and open the eyes of their employers, just as it had lifted up our hearts and opened our eyes on so many occasions.

It made a difference. Within a few months, four out of the five hotels had agreed to sit down at the table with their employees and negotiate agreements that would guarantee better working conditions. Many of them even became supporters of a "living wage" ordinance, designed to ensure that people who work hard are able to earn enough to have a decent living in that community. By practicing our faith out on the streets of Los Angeles, we entered into the struggle that eventually led to the conclusion we had all been hoping to achieve.

There is no end to the way in which liturgies can be brought out into our communities and used to bring about positive change. At CLUE we have focused on issues of economic justice, but our texts, rituals, and symbols speak to many—if not all—of the modern political crises that we face: environmental devastation, violent conflict between nations and within our own towns and cities, human trafficking, and the list goes on. God cares about all these things and has provided us with the resources to bring about transformation through our faith. We are only limited by our creativity and our willingness to live our faith out in the world, not just on Sunday mornings in our respective church buildings.

Liturgical politics is about us letting our faith engage the political process through public practice for the sake of changing our communities. It is about bringing hope into that process, including those who are otherwise excluded, and demonstrating that God desires for all of us to live in love and dignity.

Questions for Discussion and Contemplation

1 What does the way you worship communicate?

2 Have you ever been involved in a public action or political protest? What happened? What did you learn?

3 Steve Holt writes, "Every faith tradition teaches that from God's point of view a society is measured by the way it treats its poorest and weakest members: the people most likely to be kept out of the halls of power and forced to fend for themselves." Do you agree or disagree? Why or why not?

Becky Garrison

9

Vote for My Jesus

During the 2008 election, *change* emerged as the new catchall buzzword. During my recent travels, I observed what religion scholar Phyllis Tickle terms "The Great Emergence," a period of massive societal upheaval impacting technology, science, politics, religion, and the culture at large. We are entering a new faith frontier that nevertheless, upon further examination, contains the threads of church tradition woven into the fabric of the future.

During the 2008 election, I noticed a number of evangelical and emergent church leaders who interpreted this spiritual sea change by endorsing a particular candidate. While one can say that "emergent" is a conversation, once you are seen as a published author/pastor/spokesperson of any religious enterprise, your words carry weight when uttered in any public forum, be it book or blog.

Something in my bones tells me we're on the precipice of a slippery slope where, before we know it, certain groups will be perceived as political pawns. (By the way, ever notice how the same faith folks who use "Jesus rode a donkey" as a political slogan slam religious conservatives for endorsing a Republican candidate?)

This bantering by all the candidates claiming to be the champion of change brings to mind previous campaign slogans, such as "Change We Can Believe in," "Compassionate Conservatism," "Putting People First," and "Kinder, Gentler

Nation" that have been utilized to galvanize voters to rally behind a certain candidate. A quick run-through of the politics enacted during any President's term reveals that their rhetoric fell short of their results once they were in office and reality set in.

When we feel seduced into serving an earthly king instead of our king in heaven, let us not forget the story of Saul. Throughout history, whenever God's people have tried to establish themselves as earthy lords, eventually their kingdom crumbled. Even the best believers can be seduced by the lure of political power, especially if the glare of the media spotlight happens to shine on them. Next thing you know, they end up advancing their own activist agenda instead of proclaiming the Good News.

Even the best believers can be seduced by the lure of political power.

This foolish quest to conform Christ's teachings to the whims of a particular political party has really started hitting the faith, and it's been stinking up the local churches big time. I know Jesus was born in a barn, but do churches have to smell like one as well? I think it's high time we started mucking out the stables. Tony Campolo's infamous quote about mixing of church and politics should serve as a cautionary reminder here: "Evangelicalism getting wedded to any political party is like ice cream mixing with horse manure. It's not going to hurt the horse manure but it sure will mess up the ice cream."[1]

In *The Future of Faith in American Politics,* David P. Gushee lays it on the line:

> You cannot be both a party strategist and a Christian prophet. In biblical terms you cannot wear both the king's mantle and the prophet's robe. These are separate callings that are only damaged when they are mixed. This mixture is precisely what has happened to the evangelical right. Christian witness will not be benefited if it also happens to the evangelical left.[2]

When I interviewed Jeff Sharlet, author of *The Family,* I asked him how he perceived—as an outsider—how Christians should interact with the public square:

> To me it's about salvation vs. deliverance. Yes, I know, salvation has a positive term. But what salvation has come

to mean in America is the preservation of the *status quo.* Deliverance is a much stronger idea—it's the Exodus story. Instead of authority coming from above, deliverance is the idea that we're responsible for our own freedom, whether we believe God gave us that ability or we believe we're all alone,deliverance is an idea that believers and non-believers alike can embrace, the idea that we have the power to free ourselves. Now go and use it. And walk away from Empire totally.[3]

If another devout Democrat or righteous Republican tells me that they can endorse a political candidate on their own blogs (or worse, choose to blog on a politically partisan Web site) because it doesn't impact their public ministry, I'm going to throw the complete works of Phyllis Tickle at them. This Southern scholar has written more than thirty books. So I know that pelting them with her prophetic prose would hurt like heck, both literally and figuratively.

Even though the IRS says you can endorse a candidate as long as you're speaking personally and not on behalf of the organization you represent, that doesn't mean it's a good idea. How in God's name can any holy hipster claim they are representing a church or a religious organization that claims to build bridges, unify the church, and bring people together if they are engaging in partisan politics?

Let's be honest, regardless of who is President, that person will still serve as the king. Some Commander in Chief may be a more benevolent dictator than another, but the President still represents the Empire. And we serve a different King.

"SOUL LIBERTY"

When I was researching my dysfunctional family tree I learned I'm a direct descendant of the Rev. Roger Williams, the founder of the state of Rhode Island and a champion of religious freedom. The more I delve into my twelfth and thirteenth great-grandfather's work, the more I realize we're very similar souls.

So perhaps Williams' writings can provide some added perspective here. Despite constant threats of persecution, book burnings, and other means of oppression employed by the crown, he continued to advocate for the preservation of "soul liberty," a term that means that neither the state nor the church can judge anyone's conscience regardless of the person's religious beliefs

According to Williams, individual conscience must be free from the tyranny of the majority. As he noted, state sponsorship of religion would yield an unhappy situation wherein "the whole world must rule and govern the Church." The merger of church and state remains "opposite to the souls of all men who by persecutions are ravished into a dissembled worship which their hearts embrace not."[4]

Along those lines, could our Lord and Savior Jesus Christ ever be considered as a viable candidate for public office? If he were on the ballot, how many Christians would actually vote for a platform based on his teachings? Jesus can't spin worth diddly-squat. He tells it is like it is and doesn't give a rip who he offends. Even the disciples abandoned him at the foot of the cross when the going got rough. The few women who stood by Jesus hardly constitute a viable voting bloc.

If Jesus wanted to reside in the White House, he'd definitely have to tone down the Sermon on the Mount speech (Matthew 5—7) or risk losing the Soccer Mom, the NASCAR dad, and whatever other idealized demographic pollsters determined must be placated in order for a candidate to procure the political prize. After all, U.S. foreign policy has never advocated blessing peacemakers. Even under the most liberal of administrations, the least of these get left behind.

U.S. foreign policy has never advocated blessing peacemakers.

Also, Jesus' message is geared toward those "undesirables" who probably aren't even registered to vote or don't possess U.S. citizenship papers. That whole business of separating the sheep that are eligible to vote for Christ from the hordes of unregistered goats represents a pollster's nightmare. I can see the opposing party ensuring that Jesus' followers get deported or at least detained as "persons of interest."

Let's not forget Jesus' temple turning tirade. How can a political party sponsor a candidate who can't even be trusted to go to a fundraising event and behave in front of the those all-important special interest groups needed to finance the cost of mounting a political campaign? Besides, Jesus doesn't even own the right Armani suit and tie needed to gain entrance into all the right clubs.

Then you have the touchy subject of Jesus' entourage. His campaign manager looks like one of those crazy homeless guys I see preaching at Times Square, and Jesus' scandalous encounters with unsavory women would make even the Kennedys blush. He hangs out with tax collectors, drunkards, and a host of unsavory characters. And last but not least, His "trusted" disciples, the guys He appointed to key leadership positions, make snafus almost every time they accompany their leader in public. (I can just picture all the Christian conspiracy books blasting the behavior of Jesus' cabinet.) Get this—He can't even get any respect in His hometown. So, odds are He won't be able to win even the backwater town of Nazareth.

While today's politicos are obsessed with advancing their own agenda, as Brian McLaren notes in *A Generous Orthodoxy*, Jesus didn't overturn the tables "so that all the wrongs could be excluded. No. Jesus turned the tables and scattered the doves and coins so that the temple could once again become a house of prayer for all nations—an inclusive place that welcomes all into the transforming mystery of prayer and worship, not only the 'already right' or the 'rich in spirit.'"[5]

This idea may be seen as radical to those who feel that the kingdom of God should be open only to a privileged few. But this radical rule breaker and love maker broke down all race and class barriers, bringing together into one body of believers such diverse individuals as tax collectors, fishermen, and prostitutes.

Voting=Damage Control

During the "Jesus for President" tour, authors and activists Shane Claiborne, Chris Haw, and crew preached and sang to a different tune, proclaiming, "No more donkeys. Long live the lamb." Claiborne notes, "This is not about going left or right; this is about going deeper and trying to understand together. Rather than endorse candidates, we ask them to endorse what is at the heart of Jesus and that is the poor or the peacemakers, and when we see that, then we'll get behind them."[6]

Whenever I'm asked if I vote, I respond that some women paid such a dear cost so that I could have this right that I don't feel I can sit at home on election day. But like Shane, I view voting as "damage control." I go into the voting booth to cast my vote for who I hope will be the more competent person for a particular post. Simply put, I do not place my ultimate hope in anyone but Christ, for He is the true light I felt shining back in Bethlehem.

Questions for Discussion and Contemplation

1 Is it ever a good idea for a religious leader to speak in favor of a particular candidate or policy? Why or why not?

2 What do you think the role of "individual conscience" should be in making political, religious, and ethical decisions?

3 What does it mean to say that voting is "damage control"? Do you agree with this assessment? Why or why not?

Sara Critchfield Taveras

10

Working Two by Two

There's an inconvenient truth forming, just when the nation's needs—and, indeed, the world's—are on the rise. Across generations and philosophies divides are forming in approaches to social activism, stymieing efforts to make a difference.

But there is good news.

Consider Ecumenical Advocacy Days, Washington, D.C.'s annual, grassroots-based call to the Christian community. Christian advocates from across the country gather for policy briefings and worship. The conference culminates with a lobby day on Capitol Hill.

During the two and a half years that I worked in the United Church of Christ social policy office in Washington, D.C., I served on the planning team for the conference, and during that time, the number of young adults attending Ecumenical Advocacy Days rose from 50 to 250. Moreover, the dynamics in the conference changed toward something quite inspirational. Lobbyists with thirty, forty, fifty, or sixty years of experience commented that seeing so many young people invigorated their advocacy work—efforts that had become more of an old habit rather than a source of excitement.

The flipside was also true. I heard from college students who were deeply impressed by the perseverance of some of the nation's most senior advocates. A twenty-year-old student proclaimed, "I just met a woman who has been lobbying on Africa for *40 years*! I never imagined that was even possible!"

And so it is.

Unfortunately the continuing success of U.S. social activism today is threatened by two problems. One is generational. The other is philosophical. But the Christian scriptures can be read to inspire a new way of advocacy, one taking the best of generational experiences—and the best of differing schools of thought—to reignite efforts for social change.

The Tug-of-War Problem

The harmonic tones rising from Ecumenical Advocacy Days ring with marked contrast to the cacophony being played more demonstratively elsewhere. As a result the world's chief social advocacy sources—churches and nongovernmental organizations (NGOs)—are facing a leadership gap.

Sometimes flat notes are plunked out across generational divides.

Approximately 90% of all nonprofits in the United States were founded by Baby Boomers in the 1960s and 1970s. Now, with retirement fast approaching for many of these men and women, leadership deficits and difficult transitions are causing a variety of problems for NGOs. Generally, Boomers have been calling the shots within advocacy groups for more than forty years, and it's been customary that leadership positions be held by older (read: more experienced) generations until the younger ones are ready to receive the torch. And "readiness," of course, is based on gaining experience (also read: paying one's dues).

"Climbing the Ladder" vs. "Flattened Hierarchy"

As experienced decision makers seek new folks to whom they will pass the torch, they are reluctant to hand over power to younger folks who haven't "put in the time" like they did.

In contrast, but with no less sense of stubbornness, Generations X and Y—arguably raised in the most child-centric environments in history—tend to push aggressively for more power from their predecessors. "Climbing the ladder" isn't as important to them in a world where technology has flattened hierarchal structures and given the masses the ability to write, sell, or advocate in the public square with no oversight. So Gen Y is refusing to carry the torch in the same way—or is simply lighting its own torch altogether. Sometimes they do so at their own peril, as there is a tendency among rising leaders to dismissing the knowledge bank Boomers have to share.

Sound familiar, church? It should. We're in the same boat as the NGOs.

Churches and NGOs alike can no longer rely on customary rituals of passing the torch. As of 2006, Generation Y made up 20 percent of the nation's workforce.[1] But researchers have projected that now (2010) Gen Y makes up about 40 percent of the workforce. And they may be arriving with resumés thin on leadership experience—a flat note to be sure.

Age isn't the only dividing line creating conflict.

Where generational lines *are* being transcended, models of advocacy create a different divide. Sharp notes across schools of thought are throwing social advocacy off pitch.

I've experienced two basic groups in my work. I'll tag one group as the civil rights era activists. The other group I'll identify as post-Obama activists.

Civil rights era activists are schooled in the ways of activist movements from the 1960s, such as anti-war campaigns; the rise of feminist movements; the advancement of civil rights; advocacy for Native Americans, and so on. This group is characterized by: collective action (protests and civil disobedience); preference for interpersonal encounters; suspicion of government; sensitivity to diversity; dependability; process-oriented; hard work; loyalty; respect for hierarchy; ethics-driven; rigidity; idealism; the rejection of social norms. They are career focused, and they have fiercely dedicated their lives to building up the myriad of social service and advocacy organizations that serve our country and world today.

Post-Obama activists gather around a yearning for change that had been brewing in our country for years and was catalyzed by the campaign and election of President Barack Obama. These activists recognize mostly that the election of Obama is not synonymous with the end of racial issues. However, they are developing their own school of thought on advocacy based on an overwhelming sense that things have and will continue to change.

Even if we can't quite put our fingers on *how*.

Post-Obama activists are characterized by: technological dependence and high levels of usage for personal and professional lives; sociable and collaborative work styles; flexibility; value interactive processes; realism; respectful of those who show them respect; demanding; lack of loyalty; distrust of hierarchy; preference for communication through e-mail; and value for work-life balance. They are not simply sensitive to diversity. They *embody* diversity and are used to mixing socially with a variety of people. They don't posses collective consciousness of a draft or of back-alley abortions. Their context is one post-Sept. 11, 2001, where controversy about undocumented immigrants provides a puzzling dimension to racial conflicts and gay equality movements make more headlines than long-time racial equality movements.

Religiously, post-Obama activists don't have the same sense of denominational loyalty as the civil rights era activist may. In fact, the former often reject religious labels, which they view as socially divisive.

Approaches to the work of social justice advocacy differ wildly between these two groups. For example, the civil rights era activists tend to classify multinational corporations (MNCs) as perpetrators of corporate greed, rejecting the model entirely and fashioning anti-corporate campaigns, such as boycotting clothing retailer Gap.

Although the post-Obama activists may view MNCs in the same light, they tend to welcome open collaboration with the corporate sector in order to solve problems. While both recognize problems of inequality in the global economy, civil rights era activists tend to be anti-globalization. The post-Obama activists favor reform in globalization.

Generally, Code Pink, PETA, Jesse Jackson, and the National Organization for Women (NOW) are examples of civil rights era activists. Rock star Bono and his ONE Campaign, Moveon.org, and Organizing for America (President Obama's grassroots campaign), represent post-Obama approaches.

2 GENERATIONS. 2 CENTERS OF GRAVITY

In my experience, the two generational groups appear to be functioning with radically different collective consciousness, acting from different centers of gravity. In a multicultural, multiracial, pluralistic society, the framework of 1960s activism simply doesn't make sense to the post-Obama generation. Yet the civil rights era activists still hold the power in most advocacy organizations. They form forward-looking strategies based on their worldview. `

It's becoming clear that while they may have similar goals, civil rights era activists and post-Obama activists simply won't reach their goals the same way.

And so here we are: Two tug-of-war matches seem to be underway: one generational, one philosophical.

Meanwhile, people on the margins suffer in the not so heady middle, mired in human despair and a muddy future. For NGOs and for churches, there must be intentional efforts toward closing these leadership gaps.

Model Revealed in Scripture

I have reflected on intergenerational issues solely through the lens of my own political activism. While I am by no means an academic on the issue, I believe that people of faith can play a unique role within the larger NGO community to provide alternative responses to divisive generational issues: responses rooted in Christian values, including accountability, humility, friendship, and mutuality.

In Luke 10, Jesus sent his followers out two by two, telling them they were going into the world as "lambs into the midst of wolves," a metaphor particularly relevant within the ministry of social justice advocacy. Jesus advises them further not to "move about from house to house." In other words, he advocates that they stay put for the long haul—and to do so in pairs.

In Acts 13, the Holy Spirit says to the church of Antioch, "Set apart for me Barnabas and Saul [Paul] for the work to which I have called them" (v. 2b). And the two set out together and did some great ministry. Later, in Acts 15, they have a falling out and decide to separate. Yet they don't each go solo: Barnabas takes Mark with him, and Paul chooses Silas to continue doing ministry.

These passages suggest that the early Jesus movement appears to be more communally driven than individualistic; more consensus-oriented than hierarchical. Jesus didn't expect his followers to work on their own strength. He instructed them to pray and to assume the spiritual posture of lambs.

Too often our advocacy work is structured as if we believe that God wants us to go it alone. Rugged individualism is central to U.S. culture. We set ourselves up in structures of hierarchy that encourage belief in expert theories—that is, the person at the top of the hierarchy is the expert. Not only does this rob power from those below, it also places unrealistic expectations and pressure on leaders at the top. Jesus provides another model. He sends his followers out into the world in *ministry teams* of two. Many justice issues we face require long-term thinking. Typically, social issues change only after years of continual pressure. So a case can be made strongly that generational cooperation is vital to social advocacy's continuing success.

Could a buddy system that uses intergenerational strengths be helpful in our quest for a more just world today?

Two by Two

As a response to leadership transition challenges, most NGOs have focused on understanding divisions and fostering respect for generational differences. This is a good first step. Organizations must educate themselves in order to actively address generational paradigm shifts in the twenty-first century. Yet most NGOs have stopped short of using authentic relationships for reconciliation in their organizational models. They prefer to "manage" the differences instead.

Fortunately, churches can base organizational change on scripture and prayerful discernment, unlike secular NGOs. While many churches use discipleship (or mentoring) as a way to reconcile generational gaps, and while these models play significantly important roles within Christian communities, we seldom use models that pair generations in equal power relationships.

I envision a type of co-leadership model that pairs a civil rights-era-styled activist with a post-Obama one, both agreeing on a clear covenant within the model to use and celebrate all generational gifts. This is distinctly different from mentor-type models, which pair a more experienced advocate with a less experienced advocate. This is also distinct from an empowerment model, in which younger generations are empowered to take on leadership roles within an organization for which they may not yet be prepared.

Two-by-two models recognize the inherent worth of diverse contributions from all ages and experience levels as equally important and *necessary* in the process.

Examples could include intergenerational pastoral approaches—two pastors of different ages that hold the same title (not "Senior Pastor" and "Associate Pastor," but simply "Pastor"); intergenerational co-chairing of church committees; or an intergenerational team of lobbyists visiting a local government office. In this way, each person would have another to share advice, responsibility and decision making as they face the wolves that confront them. And leaders wouldn't feel so weighted under the burdens we are quick to let them carry alone.

Culturally we are so invested in individualistic and personality-driven models of leadership that it is hard to envision leadership positions being held jointly by two people of different generations. We fret about funding, personality clashes, and productivity. But we must remember that God didn't call us to have large organizational capacity. God called us to be obedient and reconciled. When we realize that the organizational process *is* the road to reconciliation and justice, we will see that we've had misplaced priorities all along. When using a two-by-two model for advocacy work, we practice interpersonal reconciliation (repentance) while simultaneously practicing systemic reconciliation (political activism).

If the two-by-two model is implemented in a place where salary is involved, the pay should be the same amount for both regardless of age or experience. This violates another cultural norm that more pay for more experience is fair. Yet this traditional business model also sends the message that our top leaders are more valuable or that they do more work to deserve more pay. Equal pay for equal work has been a justice issue between men and women for years, but is rarely addressed in the context of ageism. The truth that calls to us from the Bible's pages is that older people are valuable, *and* so are younger people; they simply have different things to offer.

Remember that the covenant of this model invites us to recognize contributions from all ages and experience levels as equally important and *necessary* in a healthy advocacy process. When Christians subscribe to capitalist theories, corporate business models, and societal norms, we are deflating our own ability to connect with the Divine and to live radical lives of Christian identity. Until Christians can put *justice in work* we will lack integrity in our *work for justice*. What better way to affirm Christian principles than by institutionalizing pay scales that proclaim the equal value of all of God's children?

It should be noted that what works in one Christian community may not work in another. Ethnicity, culture, size, geographic location, financial capacity, and mission statements of different churches or organizations must be taken into consideration when formulating solutions for particular communities. With generational issues, one size does *not* fit all, and it's important for local churches and organizations to build consensus about what is right for their own communities.

Reconciliation in Action

Finding my way on Capitol Hill was one of the most frustrating and satisfying accomplishments of my life. Government is complicated, and enacting a truly effective ministry of advocacy calls for broad coalitions, compromise, prayer, and lots of patience. I worked with some of the most passionate, caring, and intelligent people, who taught me lessons that I use daily.

However, I often felt frustrated with the bureaucracy of the church, systemic structures organized with a civil rights era framework and the widespread investment in 1960s methodology—all of which limited my contributions as a young staff member. I was constantly caught within a civil rights era and post-Obama clash. Ironically, I also watched my older counterparts, intrigued by innovative technology, struggle to let go of old ways of doing things and learn new, complicated systems. I realized that for the civil rights era activists, an internal battle is raging as well.

Representing the United Church of Christ at the Interfaith Working Group on Trade and Investment (IWG), a broad coalition of faith partners advocating for fair trade policies, was the high point of my Christian advocacy experience in Washington, D.C. Everything in that group is done through a co-leadership model.

That's how I wound up co-chairing the working group for legislative and lobbying strategies with Catherine, a Catholic nun in her seventies who had been working the Hill longer than most of us had been alive.

Catherine worked on the Hill back when Congressional staffers and nonprofit staffers had closer relationships. She knew Congress members personally and could get more accomplished in one phone call than I could in a week's worth of work. When I found myself tripping over words in our meetings, Catherine would break in with a commanding sentence that would sum up the issue. She had a way of looking people straight in the eye, and saying no to a seventysomething nun filled with such fiery opinions was hard for anyone to do. She blesses Capitol Hill with a fantastic ministry of advocacy.

On the other hand, always equipped with a laptop, I sent meeting minutes out the same day of each meeting and did detailed follow-up to hold the working group accountable for accomplishing what we agreed on. My energy often came in handy during lobbying days with long hours. When Catherine's phoning a friend on Capitol Hill didn't work, I was filled with innovative ideas we could try. The civil rights era folks in the group didn't often see eye-to-eye with the post-Obama folks, but we made a good team because the organizational structure allowed for equal contributions in leadership roles.

The Interfaith Working Group on Trade and Investment institutionalized interpersonal reconciliation before advocating for systemic reconciliation in trade justice. No decisions are made without the consensus of the whole group. This means the work can be murderously slow, and sometimes decisions simply don't get made in time to affect change. Some members of the faith community have dropped out of this group out of lack of patience with the process. The group's working methods violate cultural norms of efficiency and leadership. Like Paul and Barnabas, we often got irritated with each other. At times the inherent consequences of this model pushed the need for interpersonal reconciliation within the group to the top of the priority list and pushed the mission statement of trade justice to the back.

But the benefits of the working group's model were rich. Our advocacy was more effective because we used everyone's contributions and stronger because all the members took ownership of the work. The group has avoided the cult of personality in leadership positions, which can be the downfall of so many advocacy organizations. While the work is frustrating and slow, working two by two keeps the IWG rooted in Christian values such as accountability, humility, friendship, and mutuality. Running an advocacy marathon takes endurance, and we must depend on a strength that is not our own. I learned in Washington that sometimes strength shows itself through others around you. That group is a great example of practicing personal reconciliation (repentance) while simultaneously practicing systemic reconciliation (political activism).

We Shall Overcome

From the time we are born, our society separates us on the basis of the very divisions that Jesus came to eliminate: gender, race, culture, age, class. A two-by-two model helps heal those divisions. The civil rights era movers and the post-Obama shakers need to bridge differences, confront misunderstandings, and figure out how to work together in order to advocate in the twenty-first century. Together we can use the gifts that God gives us at every age by instituting models of shared power that celebrate generational differences.

I truly believe religious organizations are uniquely positioned to be shining examples in our society of how to *work justly*, not simply examples of how to *work for justice*. It is clear to me that if we are not working for justice and reconciliation in our own community, we will not be good messengers of God's reconciliation for the world. Utilizing a two-by-two model is just one way to proclaim the radical justice we are called to by God. Two-by-two approaches will challenge advocates to rely on their own experiences of truth rather than on firmly established corporate structures or cultural stereotypes.

There is no better time than now to follow the instructions that Jesus gave his followers when he sent them among wolves. The wolves we face today are great. But in facing them together, we shall overcome.

Questions for Discussion and Contemplation

1 Do you agree with Sara Critchfeld Taveras's description of a generational divide? Would you describe the generational differences in another way?

2 The model for this partnership is based on a reading of Acts 13. Can you think of other ways of using biblical models for political engagement?

3 What is the difference between "working justly" and "working for justice"?

wtf?

Matthew Dunbar

11

A Journey toward Justice

Shifts in Search of More Just Politics

How on earth did I get here?

I just couldn't shake the question as I occupied my seat in the third pew of Shiloh Baptist Church in Erie, Pennsylvania. Of course, it wasn't odd that I was in a church. After all, I was baptized Episcopalian as a baby, became a born-again Evangelical at fourteen, and studied theology at a Christian university. In fact, over my short twenty-six years of life, I had attended countless Christian congregations, conferences, and concerts, from Lutheran to Vineyard and from Promise Keepers to DC Talk. Having grown up Evangelical in the Central Valley of California, the conservative Christian heartland of the blue state, church on Sunday has always been second nature to me.

What made this particular Sunday so different from my previous experiences were the context and the company.

Shiloh Baptist Church is a historically black congregation in Erie. Directly to my right sat Mike Waltner, a Democratic candidate for United States Congress, and my new boss.

As we stood up and began rocking back and forth to the joyful and spirit-filled gospel choir leading worship, I couldn't help but chuckle to myself as I reflected back on the road that led me to the frigid city of Erie, in the middle of the contentious and historic primary election of 2008. Just a few years earlier I never would have fathomed that I would one day be working for, and advising, a Democrat.

"Younger Me" would have assumed that "Older Me" had lost his faith or been corrupted by higher education and years living among the godless liberals in New York City. Yet my theological understanding remains foundationally conservative. Maintaining my identity as a full-blooded Evangelical, I hold fast to my beliefs in the atoning sacrifice of Jesus Christ for the forgiveness of sin, the baptism and continued influence of the Holy Spirit, and the inerrancy of scriptures. But the way I view the world is unmistakably different from that of the majority of my Evangelical brothers and sisters.

In retrospect the transition away from my politically conservative worldview makes perfect sense and fundamentally hinges on my expanded understanding of biblical justice, my personal encounters with systemic poverty and racism, and my newfound understanding of a Gospel-centric civic responsibility.

Growing up in Visalia, California, I learned at a very young age that our family was Christian and Republican. I remember vividly my mother's reaction to the election of Bill Clinton in 1992, which can only be described as a mixture of concern and general disdain. Though I was only eleven at the time, the notion that Mr. Clinton was undoubtedly the enemy was seared into my brain. As I grew older this notion strengthened from discussions about abortion, taxation of the hardworking, and the general lack of moral fiber in the Democratic Party. By the time college and the 2000 Presidential campaign rolled around, I had very little doubt that as a Christian, my political perspective was generally nonnegotiable.

This story is not unique. Countless books describe the development of the Religious Right and the influence conservative Evangelicals had on the election of George W. Bush. The catalyst that initiated my political transformation occurred just a couple of years later.

In essence, I was shocked and awed away from my previous path.

After the September 11 attacks, and during the lead-up to the war in Iraq, I felt compelled to seek out answers to what motivated the attacks, how the nation should respond, and where the Church should stand in the face of war. Yet I was struck by the lack of engagement of my Evangelical friends and the Church at large. In fact it seemed as though the majority of Christians I knew were some of the first to jump on the war bandwagon, justifying the use of excessive force as retributive justice rather than examining violence through the lens of Christ.

Shouldn't Christians be the **last** people to go to war?

I felt a strong temptation to conform to this mentality. But I couldn't shake the uneasy feeling that something wasn't quite right. *As Christians*, I thought, *shouldn't we be the last people to be convinced to go to war?* But as I looked around, I seemed to be the only one asking this question.

As I watched the bombing of Baghdad unfold and listened to Fox News commentators glorify the display of power, I couldn't help but wonder what other issues I hadn't examined through the lens of the Gospel. Had I taken my political stances for granted as an assumption of my faith and Republican upbringing, or were they truly rooted in biblical principles? These questions plagued me for weeks until I finally committed to a long-term reexamination of my faith and politics.

Over the next three years, I went issue by issue and questioned whether or not my previously held position was based on my understanding of Jesus, the prophets and the scriptures, or if it was an assumed belief based on my familial and community upbringing or allegiance to a particular political party. I sought to gain a holistic understanding of what the Gospel says about abortion, the death penalty, fiscal policy, war, the environment, poverty, health care, gay marriage, and every other possible contentious issue under the sun.

What I discovered was that a huge disconnect existed between the way I understood justice and how justice is portrayed in the Bible.

As a white, middle-class, Evangelical male, when I heard the word *justice* I immediately equated it to individual consequences. Justice is done when a person reaps the penalty of his or her actions, and injustice is done when one gets away with wrongdoing. As a boy I was taught that if you work hard and do right, you will be rewarded and succeed. On the other hand, if you are lazy, cheat, steal, or otherwise mess up, you will realize a cost of failure and punishment.

The principle was simple enough, and my experiences throughout my educational, professional, and recreational life reflected this general teaching. Politically this understanding of justice resulted in very conservative positions on issues such as the death penalty, incarceration, war, and poverty. Bluntly put, I believed that those in prison, death row, or skid row were merely living out the natural results of their personal choices, just as war was a natural consequence of one nation's aggression against another.

Despite this seemingly narrow notion of justice as retributive cause and effect, I wasn't oblivious to unjust suffering in the world. I saw from afar the ubiquitous television ads of starving children overseas and genocidal wars being waged in countries I knew nothing about. However, to me these realities were both physically and theologically disconnected from my understanding of justice. This was due in large part to my eschatological overemphasis on living in the end-times.

As a result of my avid addiction to the *Left Behind* series and a seemingly continuous exposure to end-times preaching and prayer in my Evangelical communities, whenever I heard news of famine, plague, or warfare it never seemed to affect me that much. After all, I thought these events were all just unavoidable consequences of living in the end-times. Justice plays no role in these matters.

What I discovered when I delved into my Bible, read the words of Christ, and looked at the history of the Evangelical tradition in America was that the focus on individual justice and personal salvation was a perfectly legitimate reading of the scriptures; however, it also was extremely limited and lacked one of the largest pieces of the Gospel message: God's passion for *social justice*.

My understanding of the Gospel centered on the first of the two greatest commandments Jesus described in Matthew 22. I had been brought up to love the Lord God with all my heart, soul, and mind. But somewhere along the way, my understanding of the second half of these commands, to love my neighbor as myself, had fallen by the wayside. Or perhaps it had been minimized to a narrow understanding of my neighbor as only those I interacted with on a regular basis.

My concept of what it means to love God and neighbor stemmed from the Evangelical emphasis on one's *personal* relationship with Jesus and how one lives out Christ's love in one's daily life. This perspective, however, focuses only on the Gospel message on the "micro" level. The full message of the Gospel combines the personal call to love God and one's neighbor in a personal way with the general call also to live out this mandate of love in the larger public context. This general call is the striving for social justice.

Unlike my previous understanding of personal justice, which focused on an individual's receiving the just deserts of wrongdoing or being acquitted of crimes not committed, social justice addresses the experiences of entire groups of people living out heartbreaking social consequences for which they are not responsible.
God's compassion for these most vulnerable members of our communities is clearly expressed time and again in the scriptures through the sending of prophets and judges to entire cities and kingdoms who continue to mistreat those on the margins.

Widows, orphans, strangers, and prisoners are continuously referred to as groups suffering abuses at the hands of the Israelites when their eyes have turned away from God. The prophet Amos condemns Israel, saying they "trample on the heads of the poor as upon the dust of the ground and deny justice to the oppressed" (Amos 2:7, NIV). He declares that God despises their festivals and assemblies and calls them to "let justice roll on like a river, righteousness like a never-failing stream!" (Amos 5:24, NIV).

While some argue these statements could be interpreted as proclamations toward individual piety, Isaiah clearly articulates this public social mandate to protect the most vulnerable, stating,

> Woe to those who make unjust laws,
> to those who issue oppressive decrees,
> to deprive the poor of their rights
> and withhold justice from the oppressed of my people,

making widows their prey
and robbing the fatherless" (Isaiah 10:1–2, NIV).

These passages, and the multitude of others like them, are rooted in the underlying principle that all men and women are created in the image of God. This inherent holy characteristic of humanity requires that we treat each individual as the embodiment of Christ. In Matthew 25, Jesus tells the parable of the Sheep and the Goats. In it he describes those who truly knew him as those who provided food, drink, shelter, and clothing to those who needed them, and proclaimed, "Whatever you did for one of the least of these brothers of mine, you did for me" (v. 40).

how we treat the poor is how we treat Christ.

This passage reiterates the notion that Christ is not just *with* the poor, but that he *is* the poor, and how we treat the poor is how we treat Christ. This call to treat neighbor as one's self, and those in need as if they were Christ, isn't, as many of those on the Religious Right may try to argue, restricted to the private sector of a Christian's life.

As I sought to better understand my own faith tradition I came upon a number of books describing the history of Evangelical social engagement in America. I was amazed to find that the public call to systemic change was once a crucial piece of the Evangelical tradition in America. In fact, Evangelicals historically have been at the heart of causes contemporaries would describe as totally liberal.

During the first Great Awakening, for example, the first altar calls in America were given by the renowned evangelist Charles Finney. As people came down to accept Jesus Christ as their personal Lord and Savior, they were directed in that same moment to sign up for the abolition movement to end slavery in America.

Evangelicalism in America has a long tradition of engaging the political systems and structures in pursuit of social justice. From the abolition movement to women's suffrage, child labor laws and labor unions to the civil rights movement, Christians in the United States have engaged in the pursuit of holding up the most vulnerable in our society and declaring the image of God in every individual.

When I got to New York City and witnessed firsthand the lives of those on the margins of society, it became clear to me that many of the struggles of the nineteenth and twentieth centuries had not disappeared. Instead they had transformed into modern structural disparities that continue to oppress and take advantage of those most vulnerable members of our society. It was not until I saw with my own eyes the disparity between the low-income communities of color in New York and their wealthy, primarily white, neighbors that I understood that social, systemic injustice continues to thrive in America today.

As part of my graduate studies in New York, I worked as an intern at an organization that worked with religious leaders on social issues facing their communities. One morning, I attended a meeting of religious leaders in the South Bronx. The meeting was convened to discuss issues of environmental justice in the community. I had learned a few months earlier that the Bronx was home to forty waste transfer stations, while Manhattan didn't have a single one. This imbalance resulted in all of Manhattan's garbage being trucked into low-income neighborhoods of color.

These trucks, combined with a disproportionate number of polluting factories, incinerators, and plants, made the South Bronx one of the nation's leaders in respiratory illnesses. One woman, a Catholic community organizer, stood up and described to the group how she held her young nephew in her arms as he passed away from a severe asthma attack. Hearing this woman speak of her personal tragedy made the existence of social injustice real to me in a way it had never been before.

This child died of a treatable illness, just blocks from the congressional district with the highest concentration of millionaires in the country. Entire communities were suffering under policies that allowed wealthier neighborhoods to literally poison poor communities of color. In my continued work I heard testimonies of low-income, elderly people dying of heat stroke because of the lack of affordable air conditioning. I walked the streets of entire neighborhoods without grocery stores but lined with fast-food chains subsidized with taxpayers' money, leading to staggering rates of diabetes for its inhabitants. I witnessed the gross inequality of healthcare access in low-income communities and saw the sometimes horrendous treatment and negligence for those seeking help without insurance. I listened as communities told countless stories of mistreatment at the hands of police officers. I even saw the devastating effects of racist mandatory sentencing laws that carried much harsher punishments for cheaper drugs found in poor black neighborhoods than the more expensive drugs taken in rich white ones.

The more I built relationships with those whose experiences were so drastically different from my own, the more poverty and its ramifications became personal to me. I felt my hard heart growing softer and began to understand the phrase "bleeding-heart liberal." It stemmed from seeing the complexity and heart-wrenching realities of systemic poverty.

But what struck me the most was that these were not issues the Church could fix simply through acts of charity, serving in the local soup kitchen or passing the plate on Sunday.

I was always taught the parable of the Sheep and the Goats in the context of how I as an individual should personally treat others, and how the body of Christ should engage in acts of charity, kindness, and goodwill in order to express the love of Christ. It was our individual responsibility and the call of the Church to help the poor rather than relying on the government to do God's work.

As a conservative sold on the notion that government is incompetent and the individual always knows best, the best way for society to succeed was to get government out of the way, allow individuals to have ownership of their own resources, and allow people and businesses to govern themselves. And while this position may make sense in a perfect world, the realities of what I was observing in Harlem and the South Bronx directly contradicted my past conservative assumptions.

As a dual citizen in the United States of America and the Kingdom of Heaven, my responsibility to my neighbor cannot be limited to my personal life and relationships, but must necessarily influence my engagement in the governing of my society. If all people are truly made in the image of God, my vote and political positions should reflect this underlying principle.

Reexamining my politics in light of biblical social justice and the complex structural injustices facing the most vulnerable members of society allowed me to see politics with new eyes.

Rather than being tied down by partisan presuppositions, I seek to approach issues with the intent of uncovering which positions and solutions would have the most positive impact on the poor, the sick, the orphan, and the widow, and this provides a new standard for political analysis. After comprehensively reexamining a host of issues in the light of these criteria, I found that many of my political positions had moved left of center.

By examining my politics through a social justice lens, I found that I now held more liberal positions on the environment, universal health care, war and peace, the social safety net, economics, education, and others. Even the issue of abortion became much more complex than I had previously understood it to be. Rather than seeing abortion simply as a criminal matter to be outlawed, I now saw the health-care, economic, and educational influences that contribute to the higher rates of abortion for low-income women.

While remaining pro-life, viewing the issue through a social justice lens pushes me to make sure I have a holistic, biblical outlook on the sanctity of life and how best to preserve and honor the image of God in all people.

So there I stood, clapping my hands and worshiping Jesus next to a Democratic candidate for Congress, who also happened to hold a Master's of Divinity degree from one of the nation's top seminaries. I hadn't agreed to work for him because he was a Democrat or because I had swung to the opposite end of the political spectrum. In fact, I still see myself as an Independent. I moved out to Erie because this particular candidate was a good friend of mine, with whom I'd spent hours debating the finer points of faith, social justice, and politics prior to his decision to run for office. For the most part, I agreed with him. But more importantly, I knew he sought to make a difference for those Jesus referred to as the "least of these."

And as I stood there praying and praising in that beautiful church on the East Side of Erie, I couldn't help but wonder what our political system would look like if the most vulnerable members of the body of Christ had relationships with the wealthiest, and if Sunday morning wasn't, as Dr. Martin Luther King Jr. observed, the most segregated time of the week.

Questions for Discussion and Contemplation

1 How would you define "social justice"? What behaviors, policies, or beliefs contribute to a just society?

2 What do you think are the root causes of poverty?

3 Do beliefs labeled "liberal" or "conservative" ever come into conflict with a Christian perspective? What is a "Christian" political perspective?

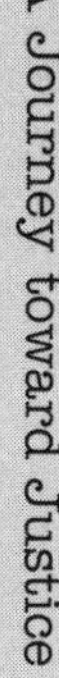

Gabriel A. Salguero

12

Defining Myself

Reflections from a Brown Progressive Evangelical[1]

Some time ago after preaching at an Evangelical conference for young Latino/a ministers in Florida someone asked me, "Gabriel, How would you define yourself?" This question certainly has a myriad of answers, but considering the context of my immediate surroundings I guessed I knew what he was asking. My guess was that the query had to do with how I position myself theologically, socially, and politically. This was a difficult question to answer in light of my cultural and ideological hybridity. The small biography attached to the conference program gave some clues to my theological and social eclecticness. I grew up as a Pentecostal pastor's kid, serve as a Nazarene Pastor, hold an M.Div from a Reformed seminary, and am doing doctoral work at Union Theological Seminary in New York City.

When I speak to a new group of people, how I am introduced leads to a number of assumptions about my identity. If they lead with "Pentecostal" or "Nazarene," I'm pegged as a conservative Republican who has made up his mind about most things. If the introduction leads with "Latino" or "Union Ph.D Candidate," listeners usually assume that I am a theological-social liberal who has made up his mind about most things.

I don't fit either assumption very well.

I know I am not the only one who, in searching to be a faithful disciple of Christ, eschews the facile definitions too often used to divide and alienate. An increasing number of Latinos/as, Blacks, Whites, and Asian Evangelicals (just to name a few groups) in their search to be faithful to the Gospel draw from a plethora of sources, traditions, and philosophies. Though we are sometimes labeled as anti-traditionalists, the truth is we are part of a long history of Christians struggling to be faithful witnesses to Jesus Christ. I prefer to be described as part of *A New Mosaic of Evangelical leaders,* or more simply, "the New Mosaics."

So who am I? I am just one of a growing group of Latino Progressive Evangelicals. I am Latino, because I was born in New Jersey to Puerto Rican parents and learned both *español* and *inglés.* I am Evangelical because I believe in the transforming power of Jesus Christ and the Gospel for the individual and larger social structures. I am progressive because I hold to the prophetic stream in the Christian tradition that says we must do better to live more in line with Christian moral imperatives. Moreover, I believe the Gospel challenges all political ideologies and denounces any obedience to any Lord but Christ.

The Gospel challenges ALL political ideologies.

What does this mean to the larger Christian church in the United States, independent of nomenclature? Simply put, progressive Latino/a Evangelicals are among a growing group of leaders who say, "Hear us, we have something to say to the larger Church." We do not say "Amen" to everything just because someone claims to speak from the Evangelical perspective. Nor do we nod in affirmation for all who claim to speak from a Latino/a progressive perspective. We understand our paradox quite well; we are usually both pro-family and supportive of comprehensive immigration reform that gives dignity to the undocumented. Preemptive war is of deep concern, particularly in light of the lives lost as a result—not just of Iraqi noncombatants but also of many poor whites, Latinos/as, and Blacks who choose to join the military. We think that poverty, economic inequity, and the environment are as important moral issues as abortion, stem-cell research, and same-sex marriage.

There is a Latino boom in the United States. We are no longer—to paraphrase Black novelist Ralph Ellison, an *"Invisible*

People." By most accounts Latinos are the nation's fastest growing minority group. This is not bad news nor an ominous sign of an invasion. In March 2004 *BusinessWeek* published a special feature entitled "Hispanic Nation." The central question asked was, "Is America ready?" Well, ready or not the Latino boom is here. About 15 percent of the U.S. population, or over 45 million people, are of Hispanic descent. Although Hispanics are less than 10 percent of the U.S. electorate, the Hispanic electorate looms large in several "swing states." According to a Pew Hispanic Center report, Hispanics make up 14 percent of the electorate in Florida, 12 percent in Nevada and Colorado, and 37 percent in New Mexico. There is no mystery as to why both parties in the 2008 Presidential election held Spanish-language debates on *Univision* and there were a plethora of advertisements running in the Spanish-language media: Latinos and Latinas matter. My passion is to make sure that these voices join a symphony of other voices to exemplify the ancient axiom *E Pluribus Unum*, Out of Many One.

Awareness of one's hybridity demands another way.

The 9 million Latino Evangelicals in the United States cannot be easily identified with one political party. We choose not to buy into either/or. Awareness of one's hybridity demands a different way. Many Latino Evangelicals have had a broader social justice agenda that is now being discussed among the larger Evangelical community. Immigration reform, AIDS/HIV education, equal housing and health-care access, urban ecology, and education are not new items on their list of priorities. The reality is that no candidate can assume they know how all Latino Evangelicals will vote. Latinos and Latinas are not a monolith.

Some years ago I began meeting with the Latino Leadership Circle, a group of progressive Latino/a Evangelical colleagues who were working together on articulating our senses of identity. We discovered that our commitments to the Gospel, to our Latino/a communities, and to a dialogue across culture and difference often made us outsiders in many groups. We searched and did not fit in in many places, so we created spaces to fit in and to speak to the public sphere.

The United States is a rainbow of races and ethnicities and cultures. However, I believe twenty-first–century politics are a bit anachronistic: though we live culturally in a high-definition world, national politics is still in black and white. Identity, especially ethnic and racial identity, becomes a means to divide people.

Undoubtedly, there is still a tendency by some in the media, politics, and culture to present the Latino population explosion as a menacing phenomenon. My colleague, Dr. Elizabeth Conde-Frazier, says that what is happening in America is often akin with Pharaoh's response to the growth of Hebrews in Egypt, "They are more than us so we should deal shrewdly with them."

Growing up in the "projects" I saw this happen too often. The urban plight often caused serious tension between blacks, poor whites, and Latinos. This tension is probably behind the question in recent debates regarding whether undocumented immigrants had impacted jobs for African Americans. Much to President Obama's credit he said the following during a presidential debate with Hillary Clinton: "To suggest somehow that the problem that we're seeing in inner city unemployment, for example, is attributable to immigrants, I think, is a case of scapegoating that I do not believe in, I do not subscribe to."

The Pew Research Center published a report asking the question, *Do Blacks and Hispanics get Along?* The response was yes, even if there are important distinctions on several issues. In recent years many leaders in the brown and black communities are emphasizing the "ties that bind" and not the walls that separate. In this new conversation any political candidate that continues to scapegoat Latinos, particularly undocumented immigrants, for the problems in this country is simply doing politics in classic, divisive, unhealthy ways. Moreover, many of our young leaders, tired of the old divide-and-conquer techniques, are seeking creative solutions and building new coalitions.

The question for these new mosaics, Latinos included, is "How are our issues spoken to in addition to the issues of others?" If candidates are aspiring to be the leaders of this pluralistic country and influence the free world, "How will they assure that there is no tyranny of the majority?" The mosaic vote does not just want a cursory nod that says, *"Hola, yo hablo español, mandarín o francés."*

Recently, I've joined an organization called New York Faith and Justice and I've learned something about a new wave of voters. Two of the prominent leaders are an African American Cherokee

Chickasaw woman, Lisa Sharon Harper, and a white Evangelical man, Peter Heltzel. Lisa and Peter are an example of this emerging voter constituency that, in my words, "get it." They welcome the brown perspective and continually want to be challenged and informed by it. Peter and Lisa are working as allies to make sure that issues important to Latinos are at the forefront of our citywide and national dialogue. This is a critical moment and a sign of hopefulness that our elected officials need to emulate. The brown voice is not a footnote. It is an intrinsic part of the national narrative. What is critical is that there not be an attempt to assimilate that voice into a grand, single narrative but rather to develop a sense of unity while respecting diversity.

So as a "New Mosaic" how would I answer that pesky question about identity?

As a follower of Jesus, I am tired of a politics of demonization and divisiveness. I believe it is critical to listen to the issues that Latinas, Asians, Whites, and Blacks are raising concerning immigration, education, economics, and foreign policy. Tensions exist, but instead of an either/or politics, we need to seek a mosaic dialogue that offers creative and hopeful solutions. The new mosaic is made up of a hopeful people who value our identities and have something distinctive to contribute to the country's future.

As a minister, I must pray and work so that this high-definition picture continues to emerge. To paraphrase Gandhi, "There is no way to this mosaic dialogue. The mosaic dialogue *is* the way."

Questions \ for Discussion and Contemplation

1 Do you think we should strive to be "color-blind" as a nation? Is this even possible?

2 Have you ever seen racial or ethnic identity used to divide people over political issues?

3 What do you think of the "New Mosaic" as a description for a generation?"

Nicole M. Lamarche

13

Pulpits and Politics

"Don't talk politics."

I have never considered myself to be a radical person, let alone a radical pastor. However, spending most of my time with people who are called "the Greatest Generation" often makes me feel like the punk kid with a loud mouth. Like many of my peers of the so-called Y Generation, challenging the status quo is not radical at all, but a way of life. Change is not something to fear, but the only thing we can count on. We find that politics is not a conversation to be avoided or an enterprise that deserves no trust, but rather the vehicle by which change happens. But I never noticed how "Y" I really was until I found myself smack dab in the middle of a village that seemed to adopt that phrase "Don't talk politics" as a motto.

Whenever I hear someone say "Don't talk politics," I always smile, mainly because I know that it is code, really, for "don't preach anything or teach anything or do anything that will make me uncomfortable." It always makes me smile, because such a statement survives only on the false assumption that the Christian faith is an entirely apolitical enterprise.

Such a phrase denies the historical reality that Jesus' death was in part political. Jesus took sides. He didn't worry too much about what people might think; he did what in his estimation best honored God. Because of that he found himself in the undesirable role of a political figure. He was political when he welcomed children to him. He was political when he healed the wrong kinds of people in the wrong place on the wrong day. He was political when he wanted to extend forgiveness to people who were supposed to be condemned. Jesus seemed to hang out with whom today we might label as "those people." We might prefer to hold tight to images of a gentle Jesus who never rocked the boat or got into any trouble. But Calvary was not a place where apolitical people died.

Calvary was not a place where apolitical people died.

Jesus did things to anger political leaders. He challenged the law of an Empire, which is itself a political act. He engaged in politically radical speech, and even in his role in God's saving acts he was a political figure.

Maybe it would be easier for us now if our Messiah hadn't been a troublemaker or a political figure, but his life and teachings show us that Christian faith is, at its foundation, political. But as much as I am willing to stake my life on this essential Christian truth, it seems that most of the folks in my town missed the memo.

Cotuit sparkles at its oft-recited label as Cape Cod's hidden gem. It is hidden from most of the hustle and bustle of contemporary America and hidden from most conversations that could possibly turn political. It was never totally clear to me what was and what was not considered "political" conversation, so I went out of my way to steer clear.

I avoided the issue until the summer of 2008, when I could no longer contain my political enthusiasm.

At the height of the Presidential stump speeches, (non)debates, and after the conclusion of both conventions, I ordered a T-shirt that prominently featured an artistic rendition of Barack Obama's head. It was a small reward for contributing to a political campaign for the first time in my life. I loved the T-shirt and I couldn't wait for it to arrive. I don't usually wear clothing aimed at promoting particular people, but I was so energized and excited, it was time to put my political voice on display. It wasn't until my shirt arrived in that big yellow envelope that I suddenly found myself in a bit of a quandary. When I went to the front desk of the post office to retrieve my long-awaited package, I looked closely to see if the woman at the counter winced at the return address. If she didn't have my PO box number memorized, I might have tried to pick it up while incognito. But in this small corner of God's creation, I can never simply be PO Box 71; instead I am THE PASTOR.

My sweet little church sits at the end (or the beginning depending on your perspective) of the town green. It rests on a holy hill of sorts and serves as a gathering place for all kinds of groups. Just across the street sits the village post office, which the church owns.[1] Further down School Street sits Mycock Realty, spelled *just that way*, and the "Kettle Ho" Restaurant. Upon first glance these two establishments raise just a bit of a smirk until one hears a local refer to the restaurant as "The Ho." It's full-on belly-laughs after that.

Not too far away sits another town establishment, my house, the parsonage. Even if I wanted to sport my newly reenergized political energy manifested in my T-shirt, I would have been sure to receive commentaries of one kind or another. I am not against ruffling feathers now and then, but my political garb invited me to ponder the world of pastoral politics. Is it really possible to express my personal hopes for the future of my country without risking the possibility that I might close some doors to pastoral conversations? Perhaps I would not be faced with such a dilemma if I were serving a church in a place other than New England. But this part of the country is full of reserved and polite people who appreciate unrocked boats. In general, politics and faith, or more accurately politics and the church, simply do not belong together. In case I had any doubts about this unwritten rule, I learned it again at a church council meeting.

Toward the end of our long meeting, the moderator asked if there was any new business. One member piped up, and I received the full force of the church version of a cable news rebuttal.

I still imagine how we might appear if we were debating in such a fashion. In one box, the dorky, slight "young woman" trying her best not to apologize but seeing the writing on the wall. In the other box, the longtime local who believes appropriateness is on her side. I sat upright with my best listening ears and heard from the committee concerned with conserving constraint about how I had crossed the line.

Mental note: Here is the line.

She and a few others shared their strong dissatisfaction that I had included a denominational letter against a state proposition in the insert of the bulletin.

"This is not appropriate," I was told. "This is not the place for politics." I quickly ruled out the possibility of jumping up on the table and chanting, "Jesus is political, Jesus is political," and when my words finally found their way out, I realized that it didn't really matter what I said. This political standoff was not so much about what I had done, but about the fact that something "political" had managed to find its way into the world of all things "religious."

Given that I sat at one end of the table and at the far end of our generation gap, I opted instead to hear the angst that they were expressing.

As I listened a question started forming in my mind: what *would* it look like to engage in political conversation in the life of the Christian church in a way that extended an invitation to talk instead of closing the door?

That night, as I walked home in the dark, passed the bar bursting with life and likely tons of political talk, I wondered where the rift had started. More questions came to mind. When did it become OK to divorce politics and religion? When did we allow ourselves to forget that the Christian faith by its birth is political? To me the life of faith is in part about transformation, which often means that a reordering of the fragile little worlds in which we live is at stake. The question worth discerning is not whether we should discuss state propositions, proposed federal budgets, or suggested plans for our government, but where and how to do so.

It's not like the sweet village I call home is devoid of political activity. One would not have to travel very far before encountering signs for or against the proposed wind farm in Nantucket Sound. It is not difficult to find what remains of Presidential campaign signs or statements about peace or security. Cars are plastered with political bumper stickers, and some houses even dare to display political statements. But all of this stops at the corner of School and High Street, where the church sits. It is as if one enters some kind of alternate universe, where the world is apolitical and everyone agrees and no statements are made that would offend or invigorate anyone.

There is something to be said for the church serving as a refuge from a perilous world, but when does our political sensitivity lead us into a world where we can never proclaim to stand with Jesus because we are never standing anywhere at all? I am not foolish enough to think that my age or position affords me more authority when it comes to politics, but I do know that our Christian faith invites us out into the world. Politics is really about how we are in relation to one another, and communities of faith can and should be first in line to ask the difficult questions of those of us who profess Jesus as the one to show us to God. The intensity with which I was chastised would lead an outsider to believe that I had masterminded a plan to host a political campaign in the sanctuary, when all I am really trying to do is to ask what the will of God is for each of us in this gathered body at this moment in time.

Our faith invites us out into the world.

To be sure, being in the world is not some abstract "stance," but an invitation to do what Jesus did and live how he lived and love who he loved. But on such occasions when the talk turns political, I find myself wondering, "Do we know the same Jesus?" And it is entirely likely that we each have fallen in love with a different guy. The Jesus I love and the one whose life serves as my looking glass to God is perhaps too dirty and unrecognizable. Maybe he is to blame. Maybe the Jesus I met in college, the Jesus who asks me to get up and move, the Jesus who challenged the *status quo* and wasn't all that nice is too unsavory to invite to church council.

But the Jesus who might not have a seat at the table in our fellowship hall is the very one that my generation finds most palatable and relatable. He is gritty and real, yet I am not sure that a pew has been reserved for him, at least not yet. Is it possible that our politically savvy generation has become more like Jesus and therefore less inclined to find him in a church?

With each year of pastoral ministry, I find that being a person of faith has become less and less fashionable. I sympathize with critiques that religious institutions have become irrelevant and out of touch. And yet, because of the Jesus I know, I feel convicted about the relevance of communities of faith. It seems as if Americans tend to maintain circles of common affinity. For the most part we hang out with people who think like us, who maintain a comparable standard of living, and who communicate using the same cultural symbols. Churches are places that invite us beyond where we would ever walk on our own. As our country becomes increasingly polarized, there are fewer and fewer places where we learn to love people with whom we disagree and whom we cannot possibly understand. There are fewer and fewer places where people of different socioeconomic groups, different generations, and different political persuasions end up in the same room. Perhaps my church will never be known as a political church, but when I look out on Sunday morning and see the rich and poor, gay and straight, young and old sharing signs of peace, I can't help but feel that we are glimpsing a piece of the Kingdom.

I would like to think that other sassy twenty- and thirty-somethings who want to change the world just might find it more possible to do in the context of a church. Politics is about people. Those of us who stake our hearts to the God we find in the Christian church know a special truth that is at the heart of politics: *people can change*. People can, with God's grace, become more compassionate and more selfless. People can become willing to put their own needs aside for the needs of those who are hurting the most. As much as church folks know that people are quirky and annoying, we also know that hearts can indeed be transformed. Being a young and restless pastor has often felt as if I am engaging in some kind of political dance, but my goal is not to win people to my side, to make them think like me; my aim is to extend an invitation to join God's side, to dare to look at the world the way Jesus did, and sometimes there is nothing more political than that.

Questions for Discussion and Contemplation

1 Have you ever been told "Don't talk politics"? Have you ever said that to someone in a faith community? What happened?

2 Was Jesus political in his ministry? Why do you think so or why not? What implications does that have for his contemporary followers?

SECTION THREE

We've Got Issues

Christian Piatt

14

Loving "It"

For as long as I can remember, I've been a pretty passionate pro-choice advocate when it comes to the abortion debate. Far from embracing the entirety of the liberal policy platform, my position on the choice-versus-life argument comes more from a civil libertarian's point of view. A few examples of what I mean:

Personally, I hate guns and cigarettes, but I don't advocate for the government to be in charge of either.

I prefer to see nonprofits, corporations, churches, and individuals take more responsibility for their own communities, rather than waiting for the government to fix what's clearly broken.

I don't want bureaucratic eyes or policies in my bedroom any more than I want their sticky hands in my wallet.

So it stands to reason that I'd lean toward personal freedom when it comes to a woman's choice about what to do with her own body.

Then I had kids.

Up until it became a personal matter for me, the debates were just that: issues to be debated. They remained principally on an intellectual level as far as I was concerned, especially since I was a guy and could never relate to the experience of being pregnant.

Did I honestly even have a voice in the discussion, based on my personal values on individual liberty?

Granted, I understand that the far right's gross-out campaign of showing posters of aborted fetuses and bloody dolls in carriages in marches and in front of clinics was supposed to elicit an emotional response in me. And it did; I was completely repulsed by anyone who would use such tools to win an argument. If anything, the propaganda backfired, pushing me further into the pro-choice column.

But all of this got a lot more complicated the first time I saw my kids on the little ultrasound screens in the doctor's office. Most folks know that we men are visual creatures, and something like pregnancy is a tremendously abstract concept, save for the vomiting partner and late-night runs to Sonic for a coconut cream pie shake. In a single moment, I fell in love with a little black-and-white blob. It wasn't even a "he" or a "she" yet as far as we were concerned, but in that moment, I couldn't imagine my life without it.

*A LOT MORE COMPLICATED

I was in love with an "it."

My two "its" are now a "he," five years old, and a "she," six months at the time when I'm writing. The first time around, I had a more profound emotional response than I did recently with my daughter, Zoe. Our experience this time made the personal uncomfortably political at the same time.

As I did the first time around, I went to the clinic with my wife, Amy, for her ultrasound. I tried to be as involved as possible the last time, and although we're on our second (so help me, this is the final baby lap in this family), I figured I still ought to do the right thing and make an appearance.

It's actually a pretty incredible thing to see your kid at about one and a half centimeters, up there on the screen, hardly developed enough to have one part distinguishable from another, but with a heart that, if it stayed proportionate to the rest of the body as it grew, would be the size of a Thanksgiving ham by the time they hit high school. It doesn't have hands or feet yet, but does sport some cool little curved stubs that make it look a lot like Montgomery Burns from *The Simpsons.*

I couldn't help but say "Excellent!" in my best Monty Burns voice when I saw It for the first time.

Now this reaction is a little different from the first time, when Mattias was still a little flesh nugget. That was one of the more profoundly emotional experiences of my life. And although Zoe is as special and amazing as he is, there's just something about going up the same summit again that lacks the exhilaration of your first climb. Mostly, I felt relief about the two points I made above. The first time, it was like counting down the days to Christmas while still being seven months out.

This time, my main thought was, *"man, I have a lot of stuff to do before this new person gets here."*

I should mention here that, being self-employed, neither of us has any health insurance to speak of, and in order to get approved for the public program, Amy had to get "official" pregnancy test results that allowed the state to recognize her pregnancy.

Great, my kid's going to come out with a big bureaucratic stamp on its forehead and forms in triplicate stapled to its tiny little butt. It didn't matter where Amy went for her test as long as they had a nurse on staff, so she set up an appointment at a local free clinic, where she could get the test and her first ultrasound at no charge.

The thing is, I had some weird vibes about this place after the things she told me about her first visit. Though she hadn't sensed anything too odd about the whole experience, I got the feeling there was a group behind the clinic that, let's say, might not appreciate that I'm a member of the ACLU or Greenpeace. Fortunately they don't ask about the social and political affiliations of the raging liberal, tree-hugging husband when you go in for your test, but they did ask one question that set my alarm bells off big time.

Most of the information they gathered was basic stuff like personal history, date of Amy's last period, and so on. But toward the end of the form, the woman asked her if she was pro-life or pro-choice.

> "are you pro-life or pro-choice?" "Yes," Amy said.

"Yes," Amy said, offering the sort of provocative yet noncommittal answer that would have made me proud, had I been there on that first day.

"I'm sorry?" the woman asked her. "Which one is 'yes?'"

"Both," she said. "I mean, of course I'm pro-life. Who would be anti-life, right?" I could just picture her pretty little pastor smile that could disarm a Kentucky militia. You just can't get pissed off at her when she does that.

"But you're also pro-choice?" The woman was catching on.

"I don't really think it's the government's responsibility to be in my uterus, no." I love this woman so very much.

The woman sighed and looked back and forth between Amy and the form. "We have to check one," she said.

"I'm not sure what to tell you," Amy shrugged. After a long, agonizing pause, the woman ticked off a mark on the page.

"We'll mark you down as pro-life. That's really what they're looking for."

Ack.

"So, this place is some sort of religiously funded clinic, isn't it?" I asked her when she brought her paperwork home, confirming that she indeed was officially pregnant.

"I'm not really sure," Amy said. "It was kind of a weird question, but I didn't think much about what was behind it." See, you have to keep in mind that, having grown up in a very open religious environment, she doesn't pick up on these things the way I do. But I was pretty sure I smelled Oral Roberts or the like in our midst.

I should pause here and explain that I have nothing in particular against Evangelicals. Hell, I used to be one back in the day. Some of my best friends are Evangelicals. My mom still is one. I think they do a lot of great things for the world, but they also really have a bad habit of pissing me off, and vice-versa.

My mom is a Southern Baptist and my dad is effectively an atheist, so I ended up splitting the difference and becoming a liberal Mainline Christian. That way I have the benefit of giving both non-churchgoers and right-wing Evangelicals the creeps, all at the same time.

My connection with the Christian Church (Disciples of Christ) came about when I met Amy, who was already serving as an associate pastor at a small urban church in downtown Denver. I was pretty sure the first time I met her that I didn't want to lose her, so it soon became obvious that I'd have to give organized religion, which I had shrugged off since my late teenage years, another shot.

We've been church nerds together ever since. I never would have thought it possible, but I found a group of religious folks who can tolerate someone like me, which is saying quite a bit, even today. Anyone who can handle my nonsense and at least still pretend to love me is all right in my book.

So suffice it to say that although I'm deeply involved in theology and church life as a vocation, I'm a bit of a mold-breaker when it comes to peoples' preconceptions about the prototypical "Christian." This makes for great fun sometimes, and other times it just makes things awkward.

My visit to the free clinic was certainly the latter.

Halfway through our "family interview" with the counselor during our second visit, after the young woman realized we were both involved in ministry, she let fly with a whole monologue about how she and her husband had been called by God to teach abstinence and something called "chaste living" to a group of youngsters in Oklahoma. Herself a teen mother who had given birth to her first child out of wedlock, she knew a thing or two about the other option, and decided it was her life's calling to teach kids otherwise.

While I respect someone's commitment to such a mission, I'm not a big fan of the narrowness of thought that generally accompanies such fervor. But for the sake of getting along, I bit my lip.

While they set Amy up in the stirrups and took some initial measurements, the counselor ushered me out into the hallway. While I waited for my turn to see the little peanut on the big screen, I could not avoid overhearing the two women behind the desk, talking about the new doctrine their church had developed to articulate "what everyone believed." This thing was a three-ring binder! Coming from a Disciples church now, where you pretty much have to just walk through the door and have a spark of curiosity to fit in, this kind of prescriptive stuff was a little too close to my old days in church.

Then it was like that scene in *The Matrix* where, all of a sudden, Keanu Reeves could see all the code behind the walls and people around him; I started seeing it everywhere:

The scene of the crucifixion embedded into an abstract painting on the wall.

The persuasive moral messages on the fronts of all the brochures.

The little message under the glass slipper at the counter that said, "Remember, Cinderella didn't do anything that night at the ball that she couldn't take back."

Double ack.

Thankfully they called me back to the ultrasound room before anyone recognized me as the gay-loving, left-wing religion columnist from the paper. I knew I had worn my baseball hat and grown out a beard for a reason. I hustled my commie butt right down the hall, back to where I would finally get to see pictures of It.

And there It was: the little heart chugging away like a tiny outboard motor, arm-stubs curled nefariously, Monty-Burns-style.

Excellent.

All the parts were in all the right places, as you can sort of make out in the image below:

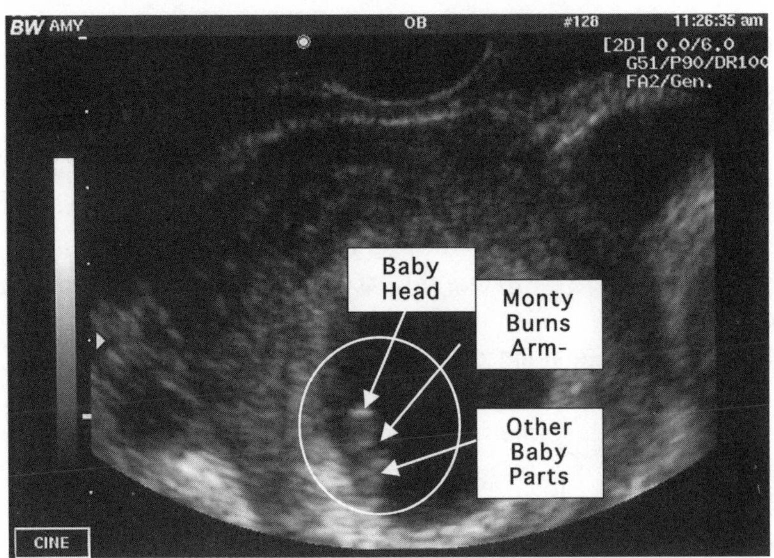

So we three are now officially four. Uncle Sam says so. And hey, who am I to argue? After all, he's paying for the thing, right?

But something else happened in that moment; I went from loving an "It" to loving a person. Nothing changed inside my wife's womb. It was all in my own personal perception.

Up to this point, I hadn't felt much warm and fuzzy stuff about this new baby. That's because for guys, it's a total abstraction until you have more physical proof. We men are fairly literal creatures when it comes down to it, and some bigger boobs for the mom, though wonderful, does not give us the emotional connection a woman has to some other living being, growing inside her womb.

That's why the sonogram is such a big deal. It's not even that you suddenly look at this little blob and see yourself in it. It actually looks more like a half-melted salamander than a human at eight weeks or so. We actually like to joke that "it has your eye," or "it has my tail," but there's no doubt it's a real live thing in there, even if it's not very person-like yet.

One thing about the sonogram that's so emotionally loaded is that the level of abstraction I've enjoyed up to now begins to dissolve. It's not just an idea or a plan for our future anymore; it's a sort-of human. Part lizard and part tadpole, but definitely part human too.

There's a part of me that admittedly is resistant to loving It. After all, loving in itself is a vulnerable act, and who wants to be so vulnerable to something so fragile and dependent itself? There's this little part of me that says *wait, let's see how this plays out, and if things go well, I'll love It.* But that's not the deal. You can't help it.

Having kids of my own, and particularly seeing them growing and squirming around inside the woman I love left a mark on me I can never erase. Whether through abortion, miscarriage, or some other mishap we were to lose the baby, I would lose a part of myself too.

So what in the world do I believe?

> "I am convinced that no one is "anti-life" or "pro-abortion."

First off, I am convinced that no one is "anti-life" or "pro-abortion." The very terms of the argument have had a polarizing effect that kills dialogue before it can start. Second, I resent either side trying to make it into an either-or debate, as if one can in all cases cling to one position or the other. For a few that may be possible, but for me, it comes down to a case-by-case issue.

I still don't believe the government has any business inside my wife's uterus, or in anyone else's for that matter. But I do think a cavalier approach to this as simply a matter of human rights for the woman is a gross oversimplification. And for all the baggage and resentments I have against Evangelical propaganda, I can tell you that their offer of a free sonogram was a peaceful, powerful tool that opened my eyes to the reality of the life we were dealing with.

And after the sonogram comes the tossing around of names, which is fun, but it's also another level of buy-in. Once you start talking names, you're definitely putting this little half-melted salamander into the "person" category. Courts and activists may debate the status of a fetus until the end of time, but ultimately, it's an emotional bond that solidifies your connection with It. No matter that we have no idea if It's a male or female, we already love It, whether It makes it all the way to the great, big world outside or not.

The most amazing thing I remember about the first sonograms is that you can actually see the heartbeat. Watching that tiny little organ, no bigger than a pea, working away to grow a life is humbling. It may look more like a sea monkey than Its parents, but it has a heart. Perhaps it has more to do with the whole romantic notion we've built up around the role of the heart in the essence of who we are, but I'm telling you it makes a big difference to me.

The mind-blowing part of all of this is what else it challenges in my belief system. I've been against capital punishment for years, but what do I do with this "dependent life" thing? And dependent lives can extend to end-of-life issues as well. I'm still all for people having the right to end their own suffering if they choose, but what if they lack the capacity or estate planning to assert their own opinion? Can one person ever make a decision that has the potential to end another life?

And what about other animals? I mean, I'm about as carnivorous as they come, but does my new life dilemma extend beyond humans? And if so, why did God make chickens and cows so yummy?

My best effort at finding some peace around this has come, in a sense, by accepting a personal and corporate–i.e., congregational–responsibility for preserving and improving the quality of life at all stages, whenever possible. Yes, I still vote in most cases for pro-choice candidates, but when I do, I establish a mandate for myself to help however I can to keep people from getting to the point where abortion is even an issue in the first place.

Here in Pueblo, where Amy and I started a church five years ago called *Milagro*–Spanish for "miracle"–we are in covenant to "give ourselves away in love to the community." This means giving ourselves to the teen mother who has no one else to lean on, the drug addicts who sell themselves for their next hit, and even to the person who is as staunchly pro-life as I may have been pro-choice at one time.

I'm not ready to jump the pro-choice ship, but the experiences of parenthood have had a permanent change on my understanding of life, the human soul, and our responsibility as joint stewards of those lives. A political candidate claiming a moderate pro-life platform no longer would eliminate him- or herself from consideration in my book. I may wrestle with this subject until the end of my days, but one thing is for sure: I love my kids, both of them. Even if one of them had never been able to join us in the world, and had never had the opportunity of loving and being loved, I would still love "It" all the same.

Questions for Discussion and Contemplation

1 Can a person be both pro-choice and pro-life?

2 Have you ever felt strongly about an issue and then had your feelings changed because of a personal event or encounter? What happened? Did you change your opinion?

3 When do you think life begins?

Yvonne Gilmore-Essig

15

Altars, Pulpits, and Priests

Losing Grasp of What's Real

The revolution will not be televised.

• Gil Scott Heron

My search for authentic leadership through the haze of media scrutiny during the 2008 election was much more complex than I expected it to be. Though I had access to all the places I had found information about candidates in the past, I did not find the same information in the same places. My e-mail box and Facebook account greeted me with data and policy explanations. SNL weighed in strongly, portraying all the major Presidential candidates in one way or another. The generations in my family were split in their support, and the endorsements of religious leaders were slow in coming and often conditional when they came. Did all the people and platforms for information weigh in because it forwarded their aims, or because it was harder to tell who was "keeping it real"? It may seem strange for me to talk about the motivation of the media, the church, and political millhouses in the same breath, but times—and activism—have changed both within and outside of the church.

For years, Americans have felt that with television, we can accomplish so much all from the comfort of our couches! We can buy anything that we need, worship, forge prophetic partnerships, and watch the real lives of other people claiming to "keep it real" all in one sitting. MTV's trailer for *Real World* in the '90s aptly told us that we don't know what we think we know: "You think you know, but do you really know me?" Indeed, life often consists of more than meets the eye. For all of the humor and joy that viewers experienced during the 2008 election season, it is probably safe to assume that Sarah Palin's appearance on SNL was arranged under less than ideal conditions. She made the best of their invitation and the persona that the public grew to know through the lens of the television. Tina Fey, the comedian who portrayed Palin, grew in notoriety. The public, by and large, marveled at the seeming accuracy of her satiric portrayal of both Palin's personality and the policies that she championed during her campaign. Was it because Fey revealed something new about Palin or because she confirmed what we thought we had seen previously?

Altars

Media often function as an altar, though they are architecturally different than a local church. Media have been altars of activism, sacred sites where civic sin has been exposed and civil disobedience demonstrated, both offered up to the public and to God for recognition and reconciliation. During the civil rights movement, images of children, men, and women being mistreated were reluctantly published in *Time*, *Newsweek* and broadcast on TV for the world see. Confirming the predictions of Martin Luther King, the images of man's inhumanity to man embarrassed and tutored the American public. Television and media at large became a catalyst for change and a kind of altar for activism that we could trust to secure freedom and change. We were a people compelled to actively transform systems of prejudice, pressured to make a new offering to God and to each other, by the mirror images of reality shown on the television, the altars in most of our living rooms.

Beyond the television, the altars that I knew, those places in my life where I sought God and offered the best and the worst of myself, were sites of music, friendship, and church. The Washington, D.C. area, where I grew up during the 1980s and 1990s, was often called "Chocolate City," because the overwhelming majority of its citizens were people of color. Public

Enemy's anthem "Fight the Power" stayed on my playlist, and A Tribe Called Quest, Queen Latifah, Brand Nubian, and KRS-One were ambassadors of hip-hop and a hope that energized me. They called for respect and inclusion and questioned the police, the education system, and a Christian faith that ignored the need for active social transformation. They were sounding boards that helped me to think through the questions and choices of the generations that preceded me and to focus on my own questions about race and faith.

I am African American and I was raised to be Christian. Nonetheless, I encountered Black Muslims, Hebrew-Israelites, Jews, and atheists of different ethnic hues in extracurricular activities as well as in school. My own questions were shaped by music, television, history books, and my own experiences of exclusion and inclusion, as well as by my church. Local politicians, including Harry Thomas, Mayor Marion Barry, and even Jean Bertrand Aristide, former President of Haiti, would visit my church on a regular basis. After a brief greeting, they would offer a word about "real life" issues faced by the common man and encourage us to vote or to become active in one way or another. My female pastor and other invited guests would regularly address issues of spiritual and social concern.

I encountered priestly activists on the altars at church, as well as on the altars around me that helped acquaint me with myself and my history. They interpreted and executed rituals to empower me to discern what was real in my life. Their concerns and their voices were deeply contextual and often loud, if not sometimes confusing, and yet I could rely on them. Long before I saw interracial interaction on television, I experienced it at church, both on days where we celebrated Martin Luther King's birthday and other times. When the police or social services didn't respond to people's need for food or assistance, I saw the church respond in loving recognition of peoples' problems and God's promise. As I grew older and struggled to discern who I really was and where God was calling me, there were priests in my midst to help me offer myself anew to God and own my capacity to see the real me.

I saw the church respond in loving recognition of people's problems and God's promise.

Pulpits

Pulpits are not new to the camera. In fact, you can watch a sermon on television any time, twenty-four hours a day. However, the kind of countercultural and political critique offered by Jeremiah Wright, while perhaps normal for some, was atypical for primetime TV in 2008. Up until a few sound bites were shared, Wright's notoriety was limited. It turned out that Democratic Presidential nominee Barack Obama was not free to simply choose his own priest. His choice was challenged from other pulpits—those of the media. A national conversation about race, faith, and politics was in essence forced by network television and a watching but largely voiceless public. Primetime coverage and e-mails circulating parts of sermons became the engine for uncovering the real Jeremiah Wright and the real Barack Obama. Pundits and reporters became de facto priests, choosing what to offer a public ever ready to consider whatever it is invited to recognize. While many chose sermon clips carefully and legitimately, what did they really expose? Active conversation and engagement inspired by faith; sin or fear; or a struggle for survival? Their coverage didn't advance the national conversation until Obama used his voice in a way that was intentional, explicit, and real:

> The profound mistake of Reverend Wright's sermons is not that he spoke about racism in our society. It's that he spoke as if our society was static; as if no progress has been made; as if this country—a country that has made it possible for one of his own members to run for the highest office in the land and build a coalition of white and black; Latino and Asian, rich and poor, young and old—is still irrevocably bound to a tragic past. But what we know—what we have seen—is that America can change. That is the true genius of this nation. What we have already achieved gives us hope—the audacity to hope—for what we can and must achieve tomorrow.
>
> In the end, then, what is called for is nothing more, and nothing less, than what all the world's great religions demand—that we do unto others as we would have them do unto us. Let us be our brother's keeper, Scripture tells us. Let us be our sister's keeper. Let us find that common stake

we all have in one another, and let our politics reflect that spirit as well.[1]

Obama's speech raises an unsettling question. Why wasn't a real conversation about race, faith, and religion taking place before March 18, 2008 when his speech aired? Why wasn't this speech planned before snippets of Rev. Wright's sermons were exposed? This controversy and the reassertion of priestly authority in the aftermath reminded us that pulpits are public spaces with the potential to be countercultural and creative spaces. Recent tensions involving faith, race, and politics, call us to re-vision activism in a way that is more intentional, faithful, and less reactive.

Troublesome Priests

The "new priests," of our time, the media, which include major networks, Web sites, newspapers, magazines, producers of social networking content, "infotainment" like *The Daily Show,* and e-campaigns are not simply sources of information but guardians of culture. They do not mindlessly re-present the events of the day but they claim to connect us to what is real.

They offer more than an unbiased, groundless, seeing eye, yet they have little or no grounding in the real aims of the Lord who calls us to seek and to search. While the media are a source of information, our grasp of the real must be rooted within and among us. When Jesus was asked when the Kingdom of Heaven was coming, he said that the kingdom of heaven "is not coming with things that can be observed; nor will they say 'Look, here it is!' or 'There it is!' For, in fact, the kingdom of God is among you." (Luke 17:20–21)

The search for Jesus in *Newsweek* or *Time* is informed by scholarship and coverage of popular controversies. Such articles attempt to guess the veracity of what Jesus is recorded saying, often without delving into the heart of what Jesus actually said. New Testament scholar Luke Timothy Johnson warns of the limits of such ventures and the seductive invitation of the media to exalt itself above truth: "The power of the media to entice participation in its own efforts is powerful, for who can resist the chance to appear as worthy of attention by the priests of the culture?"[2] Their search for the Historical Jesus is no substitute for our search and critical encounter with Jesus as people of faith.

While media priests are sometimes skilled at forcing us to ask questions and to probe what is real, let us not forget the power of activism forged through personal relationships in churches and streets, pulpits, state halls, and community centers. When the mighty flood of justice and the endless river of righteous living referred to in Amos 5:24 rolls down, I don't want to watch it, read about it, or hear about it. I aim to be a part of that prophetic flood daily and to be locally led by the real priest, Jesus Christ, not by the de facto "priests of the culture."

Questions for Discussion and Contemplation

1 What do you think of the way the media present political issues, elections, and other events? How would you change things if you ran a media outlet?

2 Is there a conflict between secular and religious perspectives on social issues? Is it a resolvable conflict?

Earle Fisher

16

The Politics of Truth

Have I now become your enemy by telling you the truth?
• Galatians 4:16

November 4, 2008, will forever be known as a monumental point in history. It was a unique moment for me personally because of the things that transpired during the week of the election. The love of my life celebrated her thirtieth birthday, as did my close friend, and my family buried an instrumental family member in Grenada, Mississippi.

During the interment, I had the honor of seeing where my family originated and a cemetery that holds the remains of my ancestors. In the midst of this emotional, yet uplifting moment in my life, I received word that my mother had been robbed at gunpoint in my home town of Benton Harbor, Michigan.

To add more peaks and valleys to this emotional roller coaster, Barack Obama was set to take charge of the nation as our first African American President. It was the moment of a lifetime. I recall watching the process that led to that moment. Information was flying in all directions about the various candidates, trying to persuade voters. Some of it was true, and some was questionable at best.

With the advent of the Internet, YouTube, MySpace, Facebook, and other sources and pipelines for substantive information and attention-grabbing sound bites, the lines between factual reporting, sensational propaganda, and outright lies are increasingly blurry. Truth in our culture has been both belittled and befuddled.

Truth has become political.

The word *politics* comes from the Latin word *politic*, translated to the Greek word *politicos* meaning "civic." So while truth was once considered to be part of the public domain, in our culture the concept of truth is just as often employed as a weapon or a polarizing tool by those in power, intent on division and obfuscation. Truth has to be sought, and in some cases actively uncovered. We have to critique everything we hear, see, and experience in order to discover what God may be doing in and through our lives.

According to James Cone, truth "is not an intellectual datum that is entrusted to academic guilds. Truth cannot be separated from the struggle. Truth is that transcendent reality, disclosed in the people's historical struggle for liberation, which enables them to know that their fight for freedom is not futile."[1] Truth has to be discovered and uncovered, which often is a struggle, but the truth must still be found, nonetheless.

I recall Pastor Frank Thomas talking about a scholar named Edward Hooper, author of *The River: A Journey to the Source of HIV and AIDS*.[2] In it he tries to trace the root of the disease. Twelve-hundred pages of assessments lead him to suggest that pathological liars are rare. He speaks to the human ability to hide truth. Most people are honest if for no other reason than because it minimizes complication—*most* people. But for many people there is a "sliding scale" of truth within which the lines between truth and lies are not so clear. If self-image, finances, family, and friends are at stake, only a few people have the integrity to tell the truth regardless of the consequences.

Hooper describes the process of lying. He says that people don't start out with a flat-out lie. What people do is dance around the sharper edges of truth, trying to come up with a version of the truth that is not necessarily the *full* truth.

Is it just me, or does this sound like our politics?

Most of us have two parallel versions of the truth: one for those we trust and one for those who might harm us. We reserve one truth for those we say we love and another for those who ask awkward questions, who have an antithesis to our every thesis and who have the authority or ability to trump our truth, if our truth is controversial. We juggle truth if it will cost us friends, finances, fame, or fortune.

TWO Truths:
1. For those we trust
2. For those who might harm us

Hooper says that over time these two versions of truth begin to blend together, until the process is completed. Suddenly, what once was one apple becomes two, Rhonda becomes Shonda, James becomes John, Tuesday turns to Thursday, and as far as we can recall, we were not ever even there at the time in question!

This is the context of our words from Galatians. The church had parallel versions of the truth. Instead of focusing on the truth, people are focusing on the politics that shape the truth, and the result is conflict. Instead of speaking to the issues, people are exacting personal attacks.

Who cares about the economy, healthcare, poverty, foreclosures, Fannie Mae, Freddie Mac, AIG, Ford, or unjust wars? People are more concerned with rock star status, how many people are coming to the rallies, and other issues that don't have anything to do with the price of gas in Chattanooga, unemployment in Knoxville, floods in the Midwest, or the crumbling educational infrastructure in Memphis.

We have become so obsessed with trivia and minutiae that we have begun "majoring in the minors." We are less concerned about Truth with a capital "T," intent on focusing more on a truth of our own creation.

And when combined with power or opportunity, truth with a small "t" becomes politicized.

I am reminded of how simply Jesus instructed the "more learned" religious leaders of the day as they continuously attempted to seduce him into a slip of the tongue. As they rhetorically attempted to manipulate a conversation to get Jesus to condemn himself by suggesting there was no separation of the role of the world in the church and the role of the church in the world, Jesus rarely responded theologically (depending on one's interpretation). Although his theology influenced his humanistic understanding, he spoke in simple language to explain how we can use our faith practically.

His kind of teaching cuts through the clutter, getting past the minor details to the heart of truth: *Love God with all your heart, and love your neighbor as yourself.* In living this out, all other pieces begin to fall into place. But for us, all too often, this simplicity is ironically threatening. In our political machines and our churches, we're more comfortable within the ambiguity of complexity.

The irony is that there seems to be an indirect suggestion that some people are not just obfuscators of truth, but actually are *enemies* of truth. Jesus came to speak truth, yet gospel writer John says that Jesus came unto his own, yet his own received him not. Furthermore, the major critiques of Jesus did not come from the drug dealers, prostitutes, gang-bangers, and thugs, but from the church people.

It's interesting how often the opponents and enemies of truth end up being the very political and church leaders to whom we look for our understanding of truth.

In fairness, most politicians and church leaders really do mean well. We have to try to do the best with what we have and still maintain regard for our own well-being. But many of us will compromise our own morality and ethical standards when our survival is at stake.

In a recent conversation with Pastor Thomas, I told him that it takes a unique and strong-willed individual to hold on to the integrity and morality by any means necessary. It seems to be a natural human instinct to lean toward the safe route and deal with the moral strain and pressures later.

There have been several occasions—one of which we are experiencing as a nation now—where those involved in the political process come to grips with the synthesis between what was promised during the campaign trail and what can be effectively implemented through governing, in the thickets of backlash, questionable support and demands from both supporters and detractors. The tension lies in trying to balance honest communication with the repercussions that can often follow. The result usually involves pruning facts and other details. Compromise is a reality of political life, as it is within any system.

But at what point does this compromise, this pruning, and this pattern of minor omissions cross over into the enemy territory of truth?

John Edwards' admission of an extramarital affair is a prime example that the truth should be told early and often because it is only a matter of time before the truth is made known. Just as in our relationship with God, we have to work at our relationship with truth. Just as Christ does not come without a cross, truth does not come without its own trouble. The baggage that accompanies truth carries its share of risks:

Jeopardy—Truth may cost you fame, friends, family, and finances. John the Baptist lost his head for truth, quite literally, as did many after him.

Jealousy—Some people will be envious because of someone's courage to speak the truth, especially if they lack such courage. Paul, in his efforts to speak truth to the early church, was not always received with smiles and open arms. On the contrary, his courage and value of truth came with its own price.

Yet if we can take a step back (a pause for the cause, as we call it in the black church), we will also discover that not everything that accompanies truth is hard. We also enjoy an enormous benefit by being a proponent of the truth. The baggage of truth also carries its reward:

Joy/Jubilee—In spite of persecution, Paul continued to preach the Gospel. Regardless of public opinion, he speaks the truth he knows. With God, truth is not political. The truth is *the truth, the whole truth and nothing but the truth.* The joy of truth is that it is liberating. With God, an apple is an apple, an elephant is an elephant and a prophet is a prophet.

People might be jealous, and jeopardy might show up, but we still must speak the truth in love. If the truth is not spoken, it's only a matter of time before we lose our minds. We might keep a job, status, privilege, or position for a while. But when we hit the wall of truth we will lose our minds. Joy comes with possessing a mind and conscience at peace with themselves. A clear conscience and pure heart are priceless.

If I don't tell you the truth, I'll lose my mind.

This is the nature of this rhetorical question to the Galatians. Paul suggests that if I don't tell you the truth, I'll lose my mind. Personally, I don't want anyone else subjected to my leadership if I lose my mind. I might fool around and forget how many houses I own. I might hire people to work with me that I don't really even know, haven't heard much about, and don't even trust.

Our challenge is to speak the truth both in season and out of season, both when it is convenient and when it is hard. We are challenged to hear the truth in season and out of season as well, and to live that truth. The challenge is to say, yes, we *can* handle the truth. Truth may be painful at first, but it's ultimately a source of joy, peace, and liberation.

I have been on a personal quest for truth in my life. I have discovered that although absolute truth may exist in the universe, human understanding of it is, at best, a small piece of the whole picture. Even the apostle Paul suggests that we all see with tainted glasses as we observe our world, and our existence within it (1 Corinthians 13:12). Each of us has to discern our own Truth(s) through prayer, study, relationship, action, and reflection.

Truth does not stop at the ideological and theoretical. Truth must be active and practical. To be spiritual is to be active and exude creative energy. We need this in the social and political parts of our lives.

Political truths may be something we're willing to fight for, campaign for, or give money to. But a personal, spiritual truth, truly embraced as a foundational tenet of our identity as God-created beings, is something to which we're willing to give our entire lives to, and perhaps die for.

Let us go a step further in determining what we would die for. Is it love, peace, liberation, justice? If so, we are challenged to invest our whole selves into that which we believe with our whole being is true, without fear of consequence.

It may be an "inconvenient truth," but then again, we're called to seek justice over comfort and peace for all over the path of least resistance for ourselves. Both the blessing and the baggage of our lives, as those who tell the truth and live the truth, is that it is our choice to make, over and over again.

Questions for Discussion and Contemplation

1 What is the difference between "truth" and "fact"?

2 Are there ever times when it is appropriate to negotiate truth by leaving out details or facts? Do you think that the authors of scripture ever did so?

3 What do you think it means for truth to be "active and practical," as Earle Fisher describes it?

wtf?

Brad Lyons

17

Crossing to the Other Side

What do you do when your faith and your profession are in a showdown? As a twenty-five-year-old journalist sworn to objectivity, I found myself covering a church in my hometown wanting to "make a big statement." What that statement actually was—witnessing for Christ, or advertising their own church—was part of a larger debate that left me feeling so cornered that it is one reason I abandoned a promising career in reporting.

In the dozen years since I covered that story I've wondered: Did my bias show? For this essay my old employer, the *Edmond Sun*, graciously gave me access to their files. With time and maturity and experience, I've been given an opportunity to answer that question.

Let's go back to 1996 in Edmond, Oklahoma. With a population of about 67,000 residents, Edmond was a typical booming suburb, figuring out how to grow into a large city while still feeling like a small town. Home to the state's third largest university, it had a significant and growing foreign-exchange student population. Edmond's high school had just split into three still-huge high schools.

Two unrelated but faith-rattling events swept through Edmond in the mid-90s. On April 19, 1995, the nation watched the Oklahoma City metro area grieve when a truck bomb destroyed the city's federal building, killing 168 people (including 19 children at a day care) and injuring more than 800. Twenty of the dead were Edmond-area residents. It stood as America's most shocking act of violence until 9/11. Faith—namely Christian faith—played a key role in the public mourning and recovery. Billy Graham led the official public memorial service four days after the attack.

A year and a half later, the U.S. Supreme Court upheld lower court rulings in favor of four residents who sued the City of Edmond, arguing a Christian cross on the city seal constituted a tacit endorsement of Christianity. The city stripped the cross and left a blank space in its place as a silent protest. Federal intervention didn't sit well in a politically and theologically conservative town, one where we prayed before city council meetings.

Every town produces an oddball kid, and I'm one of them. I lived in Edmond my entire childhood, and yet I'm a Democrat and a theological liberal.

Nearly every Sunday of my childhood was spent at the United Methodist congregation my parents helped start as lay leaders. The church quickly outgrew the pastor's home, then the YMCA, and later my elementary school cafeteria. With great pride we opened our first building, which was—there's no other way to describe it—hideous: A large box that could have been a warehouse, with Dijon-mustard siding and an expansive parking lot. Inside wasn't any better; carpet the dirty colors of late autumn blanketed the building, and the sanctuary converted to a fellowship hall in minutes. Who needed stained glass? A simple cross maybe five feet tall hanging at the front was the only sign it was a church and not a banquet hall.

What I learned, though, was that the setting didn't matter nearly as much as what was being said, taught, and done within that building. What it lacked in grandiose church architecture, it made up for in community and faith. We youth learned about other faiths, expressed our own interpretations of faith without fear of judgment, and spent the year planning spring break ski trips. By the time I moved back home after college, the congregation had taken a right turn, and my family left for another congregation, but my concept of church still has the smell of pool chlorine, leftover lasagna, and carpet glue. You could say I became an aficionado of cheap churches.

Perhaps because I was in a political minority, I'd learned to evaluate the core values of others without insulting them. And except in the privacy and trust of friends and family, I kept my mouth shut. That worked for my faith too.

Until a sunny morning in October 1996.

The city planner informed me that MetroChurch planned to erect a cross, possibly 150 feet tall. With 2,300 members, MetroChurch was Edmond's best-known and most recognizable church for two additional reasons: location (a sprawling building on the interstate at the main exit to Edmond) and celebrity (its founding pastor had run for governor a decade earlier). A new pastor had arrived in the spring, a Texan named Jim Hylton. In my mind, Hylton was the definitive Southern Baptist preacher: a rich voice, crisply parted silver hair, always in a sharp-looking suit and tie. Following in the steps of a beloved pastor who had brought the church back from the edge of bankruptcy, Hylton seemed intent on making a big splash.

A fifteen-story-tall cross is a heckuva splash.

My first thought was, *Holy cow, that's gaudy. Or God-dy.* I wondered how many homeless shelter meals or malaria immunizations the project could purchase. My church-on-the-cheap upbringing probably played a role in that.

An associate pastor at MetroChurch refused to release specific details about their project, telling me the church planned an announcement later in the week through the Oklahoma City newspaper. Public relations lesson #1: When someone from the media calls, answer the questions as best you can. Lesson #2: Never, ever, ever tell a reporter you're planning to give a story to a chief rival. I advised the pastor the story would be on newsstands in about four hours and asked for additional comments. He declined.

Then I called two city councilors, who treated it like a building issue rather than a religious matter. "Maybe if you put a couple of cell phone transmission towers on the top," one councilman said with a laugh, "it would stand a better chance."[1] Another compared the cross to pole signs crowned by fast-food or oil company logos. In a town where signs were getting smaller and closer to the ground, this was not good news for MetroChurch. That day's headline: "MetroChurch Plans Mammoth Cross on Interstate." Within a few articles, I dubbed it "MetroCross."

Eventually specifics came. The entire structure would be 157 feet tall, with a tall, skinny trapezoidal base supporting a white concrete cross, complete with lighting. The height was necessary, the church said, to lift the cross above the tree line.

What MetroChurch envisioned as a unifying symbol actually polarized the community, at least those who cared to talk about it. It seemed there was no middle ground; you were for the cross, or against it. The bureaucratic language of zoning framed the debate: The cross was either a building since it had a prayer chapel in the base or a pole sign advertising the church. Translation: "I like it," or "I hate it."

Public meetings about the cross felt like revivals, complete with "Amens" and lots of supporters quietly backing their pastor.

"We didn't set out to create the world's biggest cross," Hylton said at one meeting. "There would be room for negotiation as long as it meets the objective of making a statement. There are ways to make big statements and ways to make little statements. We intended to make a big statement."

What was that statement? I look back at those articles, and I don't see it. I'm sure I would have included it had MetroChurch ever defined their statement. The closest I ever got was a quote my wife, a seventh-grade English teacher at the time, passed along from one of her more evangelical students: "If that cross saves one soul, it's worth it." That student's opinion seems the epitome of evangelicalism, and yet that statement clashes in so many ways with my faith, a faith that believes in grace and universal forgiveness and ecumenism and a pan-theology that unites us across our differences.

So I acknowledge my key mistake: I never made a concerted effort to get MetroChurch's side of the story. I have lots of reasons (you might say excuses) why this didn't happen, namely the workload of a mid-size newspaper reporter. I also wasn't thrilled about sitting down with MetroChurch officials and listening to them explain their proposal. To me, the cross seemed like a colossal waste of money, and I didn't really care to be the public relations firm for an evangelical church. In my defense, MetroChurch didn't return my calls either. When we crossed paths, they were polite but clearly wary of me. They would probably have said the same of me. That awkward relationship certainly didn't help my reporting.

I think it didn't help their cause, either, but maybe it did. Evangelicals seem to rise to the occasion when they're cornered, when they perceive society is against them.

I wasn't the only one in a tight spot. Candidates running for President routinely endure discussions about their faith. Not so for city council candidates. City representatives who had gone on the record against the cross told me they had received harassing phone calls questioning their faith.

"I've been threatened, cussed out," one councilman said. "My secretaries have been answering the phones a long time on city issues, and they agree with me that the calls (supporting the cross) have been by far the most hateful we've received."

Hateful?

"People have questioned my faith," said another councilman. "That's not their business. That's an issue for me only. That part of this debate has been really upsetting." Hylton quickly offered a public apology to the council.

When the city council reviewed MetroChurch's plans, the normally passive mayor spoke fervently in favor of the cross, while the councilors who usually led conversations spoke cautiously. Meanwhile, a MetroChurch member, also an attorney, warned that nixing the proposal denied the church its constitutional rights, insinuating a potential lawsuit. Despite that veiled threat, the city council voted 3 to 2 against the cross, arguing it was a sign, not a building or a steeple, and therefore not allowed under city building codes.

Following the vote, Hylton spoke of love and forgiveness and acceptance of the decision. "I am surprised and I'm disappointed, but I'm not upset," he said. "We'll go back and rethink our options and go from there." Later that month, MetroChurch shortened their cross by ten feet and took steps to bring it back to the council for another vote.

That's when politics kicked in. Here are just a few articles over the next few months:

- A GOP state representative planned legislation stripping cities of the power to limit the height of religious structures. He compared the city councilors against the bill to "atheists, devil worshipers, (and) evolutionists." Under fire from fellow Republicans, the bill was withdrawn.

- A nearby restaurant, The Sellars Crab and Steak House, submitted plans to build a 137-foot-tall pole sign topped with a monstrous crab. Seriously.
- You know how every town has its own local loony? Ours loved the idea so much she lugged a life-sized cross down the main road through town and into the newspaper office. I immediately scheduled an important meeting with a cup of coffee on the other side of town.
- Zoning! Classifications! Acronyms! Don't miss drama and excitement of a Special Zoning Commission review of the I-35 corridor! Tonight at 7 p.m. on the Edmond Channel! (No, not an actual ad, but yes, an actual commission.) MetroChurch agreed to hold its proposal until the I-35 commission finished its work, at least that's what everybody thought for a few months.

One winter Sunday morning, as I listened to the sermon at my own church, I unintentionally went on the clock. "What if Jesus walked into an Edmond City Council meeting?" the extremely liberal pastor asked. There's nothing like nearly being mentioned accidentally in a sermon. His eyes bugged out when I told him I worked for a local paper. I think he was pleased.

That prompted me to call pastors around town for their thoughts. Hylton told me the religious community in Edmond was "highly in favor" of the plan, but I decided to check for myself. Several pastors discreetly asked to be left out of the discussion, while others chose their words carefully, afraid of picking a fight. I couldn't get a single pastor to go on the record against the cross; the closest I got was a minister noting that pastoral duties—counseling, supporting the ill, enriching his church's ministry—were his focus. I remember being disappointed that I couldn't get anybody with the courage to stand up to MetroChurch. With hindsight, I know that's my own bias at work.

Biding their time, MetroChurch knew city elections three months down the road would give them an opportunity to change the balance of the city council. Two members of the council, one on each side of the debate, faced reelection. One race pitted an incumbent, Gary Moore, against a cross opponent who served as a pastoral assistant at our local Catholic parish. In the other race was Charles Lamb, who voted against the cross, believing it was a pole sign. He faced a pair of opponents, both of whom had cited the cross as a reason they entered the race. Lamb narrowly won the primary and faced the genial but politically unknown Bob Huggins. *The Sun*'s owner and publisher, always wary of the power of religion, endorsed Lamb.

Election Day was April Fools' Day, and the voters of Edmond played a huge prank. First they forgot to show up, with just 3,400 casting ballots, less than 10 percent of eligible voters. Then Huggins beat Lamb. By six votes.

That evening I went to Bob Huggins' victory party: a few of his buddies in a booth at Denny's. One of them tried shoving paper napkins in my shirt pocket. "Now your boss'll have something to wipe away his tears," he said. The next morning, still fuming at this abuse and arrogance, I wanted to write about the harassment I'd endured, but my editor decided we needed to be on good terms with the new councilman, the swing vote on the MetroCross. (For the record, after winning the race, Huggins donated his leftover campaign funds, $417, to MetroChurch.)

I recall grousing for several days about the results, bemoaning the loss of a good source, and quietly mourning for my town. I also remember feeling foolish in my belief that a significant chunk of residents cared about city politics. I wondered if I had wasted a lot of time and newsprint. I also wondered if I'd be able to keep my sanity and my dignity in a town that would let the towering cross cast its shadow on the community's front door.

As I wondered, though, I knew my own change was on the way. Two weeks later I stunned my editor and my family by accepting a webmaster's job in Tulsa. With two weeks to work on my final story, I had nothing to lose. On my last day I turned it in to my editor, packed my stuff, and ended my career as a reporter.

Sunday morning's front-page headline read "MetroChurch Pastor's View in City Vote Questioned." It focused on Hylton's pastoral letter in the congregational newsletter. "Gary Moore has taken a very progressive approach...[and] has taken a strong stand to be a friend to our church," Hylton wrote. "[Huggins] has also taken a clear position in favor of our right to build the cross on the basis of our constitutional rights." He urged members to vote for "progressive" candidates. The two cross opponents weren't mentioned.

In federal tax law, a congregation's tax-exempt status also qualifies an individual's donation as tax-deductible. In exchange, congregations agree to stay out of endorsing candidates. Pastors or boards can talk about issues and even endorse ballot measures, but they can't say, "Vote for Gary and Bob."

So did Hylton's column cross the line? I'm not sure, and neither were the experts. The article I wrote reached far and wide for opinions. Naturally Hylton saw nothing wrong. The IRS refused comment, citing disclosure laws. A philanthropy expert in Indiana believed MetroChurch was in the clear. "It does not look like a violation, though it looked, walked, talked, and waddled like a political statement. [Hylton] obviously thought very carefully about this." Another expert from Houston noted, "If the predominant purpose was to recommend one candidate over another in a certain way, (the IRS) would have to look at that."

A month after the tax article, Americans United for the Separation of Church and State called on the IRS to investigate MetroChurch. They also alleged the church distributed pamphlets from the conservative Christian Coalition prior to the 1996 Congressional elections. The IRS regulation that kept them from commenting on the original story is also why I don't know whether an investigation occurred or what the probe's result might have been.

This much I do know: The story stuck with me. I followed it from a distance. In June, claiming they had never agreed to wait for the I-35 panel's final report, MetroChurch submitted plans for a cross measuring 137 feet. On a hazy summer night I drove the ninety minutes from Tulsa to Edmond to witness the final vote on MetroCross. I arrived late, but when I walked into a packed room, people who recognized me gasped. They didn't understand

I was merely a spectator, coming to see the end of a crazy story. The journalist in me won out, and I kept my opinions to myself. Though I expect I scowled at Reverend Hylton.

The new city council approved the cross 3 to 2, and MetroChurch celebrated. Minutes later, the crab sign was unanimously rejected. The restaurant owner filed suit against the city the next day, but eventually the suit was tossed.

With the issue settled, MetroChurch broke ground in November 1997. I broke ground on a novel that dealt with a small-town church wanting to build a huge cross based on visions of a grandiose future (with a lot of fiction thrown in), and I got several hundred pages into it before I moved on. A decade later, I still think it's a good story; someday I may revisit it.

Two years after I broke the story, MetroCross was completed and dedicated, and I had moved to St. Louis. The next time I went home, I arrived after dark and was greeted by the mammoth cross, outlined in sky-blue neon against a star-filled sky.

MetroCross has since merged with a nationally recognized, influential congregation and Jim Hylton has moved on. The cross is still there, though I'm told it's not lit as often as it used to be.

"I hope we'll eventually tire of ignoring our opponents."

I reflect on the experience, and it's not pretty. I see a church that pushed the limits of the law to get what it wanted. I see a city that emphasized citizen involvement, only to see it evaporate at the polls, allowing a vocal, organized minority to skew an election. And I see a young reporter who didn't try as hard as he could have to learn what the other side was thinking.

Did this reporter let his own opinion slip in? I talked to my former editor, who says my work was clean, that we kept our neutrality. But all editors defend their neutrality. Fellow reporters at the time are tainted both by friendship and by newsroom conversation. Like everything else in this story, it's a gray area. I honestly don't know.

I also see the value of crossing bridges. Americans love being right and hate being told they're wrong. Most of us are comfortable with our beliefs and our faith, and we don't like having them challenged. The other side gives us the willies. We argue out of habit. It's too easy and too comfortable to look at those different from us and deem them wrong, to stick our fingers in our ears and sing hymns or praise songs until we drown them out.

I hope we'll eventually grow tired of ignoring our opponents. We have elected a President with the hope he will transcend differences, and we need to apply that hope to our faith and to our congregations, whether it's ecumenical and multifaith discussions or arguments across the conference-room table of our congregational board meeting. Even if we don't like the song they're singing, we must hear the other side—we must understand it and respect it even though it makes us uncomfortable—if we're ever going to live into the faith God calls us to live.

Questions for Discussion and Contemplation

1 Do you think it is possible to be objective when discussing a political issue? Is there a difference between being "fair" and being "objective"?

2 Have you ever encountered political bias in news reporting? How would you describe the bias?

3 Are there limits to free speech or religious practice?

Sue Gaeta

18

One Generation at a Time

Health Care and Other Reforms Start at Home

I strive to integrate what is important to me into my life. There is a saying that comes out of the feminist movement that the personal is political. Through personal story comes political action. Reflecting on how I have received access to health care I recognize that access has been limited and considered a privilege for the wealthy and connected. I cannot tell my story without talking about the role of religion and faith. And I cannot talk about faith, politics, and health care without telling my story.

I am the child of two pastors. One went the traditional route, more or less, and entered seminary right after graduating from college. The other first had a threefold career as nurse, pastor's wife, and then mother. She started taking seminary classes part-time when I, the younger of two kids, began kindergarten. When I was in seventh grade she graduated and was ordained. So church, and even faith, have always been present in my life through my relationships.

Growing up I knew that every four years my parents did their civic duty and voted for President. Somehow, though, I knew not to ask how they voted. Perhaps I did once and was not given an answer. Maybe my intuitive sense just knew that this was a private matter. As a young adult, developing a political consciousness of my own, I pressed my dad on the matter. My recollection is that he explained that if he told me (as a child) I might go running around telling everyone in the congregation, and he didn't think that was a wise thing to do. Satisfied at the time, I didn't pursue the conversation further.

Now, as a pastor myself, when parishioners ask me about my political opinions, I'm inclined to be pretty forthright but clear that they are my personal opinions. I try my best to articulate how my faith informs these decisions as well. I have been able to have very respectful conversations with parishioners who hold differing viewpoints and not have to hold back what I believe. It is possible to do this both because I am a very different person from my parents, and also because we live in very different times.

Politics is about more than just which President we vote for. My mom used to be very active with Bread for the World and wrote letters to elected officials about hunger issues. My dad was arrested and put in jail with several other pastors for protesting against apartheid in South Africa during the 1980s. But now it seems as if their involvement doesn't go much beyond dinner conversations, a few scripted e-mails sent with the push of a button, or signing electronic petitions. At the same time, it still remains a topic that I feel a little uncomfortable discussing with them.

My parents have always been *uber* supportive of me, even if they don't necessarily agree with my decisions or actions. Mostly that's been great, but sometimes I wonder if they are holding back their opinions. I'm the kind of person who thinks she wants to know where other people are on issues. I am pretty aware of my parents' opinions of others, though, especially those of our most recent President. My dad tended to go off on rants about this or that, but I didn't get a sense that he did much more. It has been fascinating, in fact, to hear such open opinions about political matters.

One way my parents' support showed when I was a child was in their diligence around my health. I had common things such as allergies, asthma, and accidents. But I also had a rare skin condition called morphea. They took me to countless doctors and went through endless struggles to find out what was wrong.

It began with a patch of whitish skin on my hip. The doctors took a biopsy, and it formed a keloid (a bumpy, rough scar).

Then we moved on to a skin graft to get rid of the keloid so that the movement of my right hip would not be compromised. The patches began to spread. Wherever they were I could not sweat; there was no protective fat, and the muscles atrophied. Eventually we discovered that my legs were growing at different lengths as well. Since I was adopted as an infant from Korea, we had no biological family history to help with any diagnosis.

When the doctors recommended a procedure to stop the growth in my femur in the longer leg so that when I finished growing they would be even, the growth charts they had were not applicable to Korean girls. They only knew how to estimate based on U.S. growth charts. I was not on the chart. So my mom figured out how to write to a Korean doctor to obtain the necessary information. I'm glad she was a nurse so she knew how to stand up for me and not let questions go unanswered. She could wade through the medical jargon and get the best answers she could.

We were solidly middle class, so we had the capacity to travel to specialists who continued to look at my case and shrug, declaring there was nothing to be done. We could afford the lifts that had to be put on each right shoe, much to my dismay. I believe that because of being clergy, my parents received special treatment when it came to working out payment arrangements for chiropractic care. I can only imagine how much time, effort, and energy it took to tend to my medical needs—and money.

Now, as an adult responsible for my own medical care, I have a better sense of what sacrifices my parents had to make. For a simple fifteen-minute follow-up visit with a rheumatologist who knows something about my rare condition I have to pay $178, with insurance. After leaving parish ministry, in order for me to maintain my insurance coverage I have to pay $556 a month for my coverage instead of paying rent. I currently have no regular income and am living with friends across the country for as long as they will have me. I could have found a job just to pay the rent, or taken one just for the insurance. But I have more important work to do.

As a pastor, I have been shaped by congregation-based organizing and have become the president of the Gamaliel National Clergy Caucus (GNCC). Gamaliel is a national power network of faith institutions working on local, regional, and national issues. We strive to be a means through which ordinary people can grow in leadership and impact the world around us. We learn to engage the power structures, whether local, state, or national. We know that the world "as it is" is not what we are stuck with, and I have a vision of the way the world should—and could—be.

We mine the often-hidden riches of our various faith traditions for guidance and direction toward a community where each person is living the fullest life possible. Community is an understanding that our lives are interconnected. Organizing is based on building "power-with" through organizing people and money through relationships.

Community is an understanding that our lives are interconnected.

Each spring clergy and other religious leaders gather for a training and time for spiritual reflection. In 2006 we began to plan what we could work on together that would help to bring all voices to the table and be a strategic issue for building national, as well as local, power. Our 2007 national training was titled "Organizing for Love of God and Neighbor." We had three speakers from partner organizations on a panel about universal health care. They each shared some of their strategies and generated some interest.

The personal story of one of our own leaders seemed to galvanize the energy in the room. As he shared his story of how the current health care system is broken, working for reform was no longer something that we were doing solely on behalf of others; it was something that each of us personally had a stake in.

The failure of our current health care system (even for people with insurance) was something that we could all personally relate to. I thought about the piles of paperwork that covered our kitchen table when I was a child just so we could figure out what was going on with me. I know that my family had health insurance through the church, but as a child I didn't have any concept of what kind of expenses were involved, even before these outrageous co-pays, deductibles, and excluded procedures. I just knew that if I needed to go to the doctor, I could.

The first step in organizing a national network to work together was to obtain buy-in from the whole. The GNCC developed a theological statement called "For the Healing of the Nation" to share with local affiliates and use as a beginning point for conversation. Leaders shared stories with one another and debated how best to take action. We took a look at our language and chose to talk about comprehensive health care reform rather than universal health care, because of how some words are just too loaded.

The national Gamaliel Council of Presidents voted to declare health care as a national issue in the fall of 2008. This didn't mean that affiliates in all of our twenty states would work on this national issue, but it meant that we had enough people doing work already. Some were working on the state level. Others were waiting to see what happened nationally. Some were staunchly single-payer advocates. Others were going for what they considered to be winnable. But there was no disagreement on one thing: Our health care system is broken, and we want to be part of fixing it.

In early 2009 we began conversations internally, and with other groups working on reforming health care, about timing for action in D.C. We envisioned prayer services, Congressional visits, and lots of people. Now that there was an administration in the White House that we could work with, it was time to put feet on the ground.

Some of our organizers and leaders were not used to doing work in tandem with other groups. This national issue presented a tension between local and national efforts. To be true to organizing, this could not simply be a top-down, click-here-and-send-a-letter-to-your-senator campaign.

Don't get me wrong; quick electronic turnaround can be effective. But the strength of organizing is in real stories, told with passion and confidence to the people who are accountable to us. Good organizing requires capturing the power of story and making the personal political. It is not cookie-cutter, purely results-oriented work. It's about action and reflection, grounded in our very core of being as people inextricably connected to one another by a force greater than us. As a Christian, for me it's about being the body of Christ, fully human and fully divine, present in the world in flesh and blood.

On Wednesday, June 24, 2009, buses pulled up in front of the Lutheran Church of the Reformation just east of Capitol Hill in Washington, D.C. Many of the riders had been on these buses all night from as far away as Minnesota. About 500 people were present from twenty states clad in red T-shirts that read, "Faith and Democracy." We were fed and had a chance to gather ourselves. We prepared for visits to our senators and representatives later that day. We sang and prayed together. We heard from people encouraging us that this was indeed the time to make something happen that has never happened before.

Professor Peter Edelman from Georgetown Law, spouse of Marian Wright Edelman who founded the Children's Defense Fund, brought over forty years of history into the room. He has been part of this struggle through several administrations and worked closely with Robert F. Kennedy. In 1997 Edelman resigned from the Clinton administration in protest of his failed welfare policies. Three of our own people gave us the rundown on the messages about health care reform needed, strategies for a public insurance option, and the opportunities we might have to speak on immigration and transportation.

The Rev. Dr. James Forbes sent us off with a powerful declaration that it was time, because the Holy Spirit was telling us so.

The senate buildings were crawling with the red shirts and large groups that took up the hallways as we were waiting to speak with legislators and their staffs. My delegation from Wisconsin felt somewhat marginalized because we got "stuck with" staffers, and our senators were not able to meet with us. But it was an important learning experience regardless. Both senators are generally supportive of what we are asking for in a public option for health insurance so that *all people* in the United States have quality, affordable, and accessible health care. But it is just as important to thank and express support for people who are already on "our side" as it is to challenge those with different views. We heard over and over that "the devil is in the details," so the work continues as we monitor, and give our feedback to, the various committees and what they are working out, often behind closed doors.

In preparation for this day of action, leaders in Gamaliel were asked to make declarations of how many people we thought we could get to Washington, D.C. to make the biggest impact. As I thought about the people with whom I am in relationship and guessed about their availability and willingness to be politically active, my parents came to mind for the first time. The personal becomes political. I would invite them to enter into this part of my life not from afar, but to be with me.

After some quick calculations and mental adjustments, I publicly declared that I would be responsible for twenty people turning out. These would not just be people from my own organization, but those with whom I had personal relationships, including my parents. Those who heard this statement did not know the internal tension I felt about it. But I knew that I had work to do. At first my parents were receptive and even enthusiastic. But as the time got closer and my mom was recovering from ankle and knee problems, it became clear that they would not be able to make the trip. I asked my dad if he could come even without my mom, but he declined. Once again, I did not press him.

I still was able to bring out the number of people I committed to bringing from the D.C. area, but my parents were not there. I felt like I had taken a risk and been let down. This was somewhat of a new experience for me. I have always been able to count on my parents, but because of limitations of poor health they could not carry through as they and I wanted.

Was it because they didn't care? No. Could a better health care system have led to my mom being in better health? Probably. Did I convey to them how much it would mean to me personally for them to be there? No. Will I continue taking risks to bring the personal more into the political sphere? With the help of God.

Faith is a practice.

Many of the values that I hold come from my experience as a young child. Sitting in worship Sunday after Sunday taught me that faith is important, even if I'm not feeling a desire or emotional connection. Faith is a discipline, a practice, a way of opening up for the Spirit to move unexpectedly. Witnessing my parents continue to root for the "losers" taught me that doing what is right is not always the most popular thing.

Hearing the story of Jesus, who winds up being murdered for challenging the status quo, taught me that faithfulness will not always lead to immediate gains. In my adulthood I continue to have my values shaped by experience. But I also want to shape my experience as a response to my faith.

There is still a lot to do to make sure that real reform in our health care system happens. I believe many of the values of our faith traditions compel us to live our personal faith politically in the public arena. I felt so strongly about this that I resigned from my call as a congregational pastor so that I could have a broader impact. I knew that I wanted to invest myself in this work, but in a healthy way, so I couldn't be working the equivalent of two full-time jobs. I lined up friends across the country willing to house and feed me for a while. I found ways to make enough income to pay for health insurance. I moved my stuff out of my apartment and into my car. I've been on the road for four months now. Why didn't I just get a job related to health care reform? I needed time to reflect on my story and how it informs the work into which I'm called.

The work on health care reform is about more than just policies and programs. The hardest work in organizing is inviting people into a new way of thinking about their lives and the world around them. It is convincing people that their stories matter, that *they* matter. My story is about employing the personal relationships in my life toward something greater. It is about meeting the challenge to risk being let down, but never to give up.

God's promises call me into a life based on trust. Health care is only one issue that calls for making the personal political. It is only one of the pieces of my story that connects me to others. But it is part of a larger system that holds up profits over people, denying our inherent connectedness and mutual accountability. We have to begin somewhere, though. When all the issues are overwhelming, we can begin by telling our stories, prayerfully seeking our own starting point.

Questions for Discussion and Contemplation

1 Should access to health care be a political issue? Why or why not? Should it be a religious issue? Why or why not?

2 Do you think the health care system still needs reform? If so, how would you reform it?

3 What do you think of the organizing model Sue Gaeta describes? What are its benefits? What might be its limitations?

Brandon Gilvin

19

Polyester white trash made in nowhere
Take this shirt and make it clean.
• U2, "Yahweh"

Moses was keeping the flock of his father-in-law Jethro, the priest of Midian; he led his flock beyond the wilderness, and came to Horeb, the mountain of God. There the angel of the *Lord* appeared to him in a flame of fire out of a bush; he looked, and the bush was blazing, yet it was not consumed. Then Moses said, 'I must turn aside and look at this great sight, and see why the bush is not burned up.' When the *Lord* saw that he had turned aside to see, God called to him out of the bush, 'Moses, Moses!' And he said, 'Here I am.' Then he said, 'Come no closer! Remove the sandals from your feet, for the place on which you are standing is holy ground.' He said further, 'I am the God of your father, the God of Abraham, the God of Isaac, and the God of Jacob.' And Moses hid his face, for he was afraid to look at God.

Then the *Lord* said, 'I have observed the misery of my people who are in Egypt; I have heard their cry on account of their taskmasters. Indeed, I know their sufferings, and I have come down to deliver them from the Egyptians, and to bring them up out of that land to a good and broad land, a land flowing with milk and honey, to the country of the Canaanites, the Hittites, the Amorites, the Perizzites, the Hivites, and the Jebusites. The cry of the Israelites has now come to me; I have also seen how the Egyptians oppress them. So come, I will send you to Pharaoh to bring my people, the Israelites, out of Egypt.' But Moses said to God, 'Who am I that I should go to Pharaoh, and bring the Israelites out of Egypt?' He said, 'I will be with you; and this shall be the sign for you that it is I who sent you: when you have brought the people out of Egypt, you shall worship God on this mountain.'

But Moses said to God, 'If I come to the Israelites and say to them, "The God of your ancestors has sent me to you", and they ask me, "What is his name?" what shall I say to them?' God said to Moses, 'I *AM WHO* I *AM*.' He said further, 'Thus you shall say to the Israelites, "I *AM* has sent me to you." ' God also said to Moses, 'Thus you shall say to the Israelites, "The *LORD*, the God of your ancestors, the God of Abraham, the God of Isaac, and the God of Jacob, has sent me to you":

This is my name for ever,
and this my title for all generations. (Exodus 3:1–15)

He worked on a farm
He had traveled up from
Mexico

To Tennessee.
He did whatever
He was asked
For however long
He was told to do it.
There was no money to send back yet.
The tiny wage from the long hours he spent
Went to pay off the $4000 debt to the coyote who brought him across the border
But once that was paid off
After the rent and the food costs were paid, maybe there would be something

It was a rainy afternoon
Work was called off early
They loaded into the back of a pickup truck
The truck—driven by the farmowner's son—was going
Probably a bit too fast,
hit a rough spot on a hill
and he went flying.

He hit his head
His breathing stopped.
Or was too shallow to hear or feel
In the middle of a rainstorm
In the middle of a panic

The farmowner's son didn't know
What to do.
He saw a dead body.
An undocumented dead body.
So he got two other workers to help him.
They got chains.
They wrapped them around his body.
They threw the body into a pond
And it sank
Just like a rock.

When the incident was reported
Weeks later
When the Coroner examined
The bloated body of this man
They determined that it was not the head injury
That killed him

He drowned.
He sank

Just like a rock
And drowned.
If he cried out
Would anyone even hear?

—

"Slave" isn't a word we're really accustomed to taking seriously much anymore.

If anything, we acknowledge it as a painful part of our history
That the Emancipation Proclamation
And Civil War took care of.

But the fact of the matter is
There are 27 Million People enslaved in the world today.

When I lived in Kenya
In my office,
We would hear stories
Repeated all the time
About recruiters who came to little villages
With stories of well-paying jobs
Or schools
For children and young women
In the big city
"Your child will send money home. Here's an advance. More will come."
But it never does

Instead, that child becomes one of the
27 Million men, women, and children
Trafficked from the village to the city
Trafficked from the third world to the first.
Bonded to pay for the advance paid to their family
Sold like cattle
Beaten and abused into submission
Used like farm equipment
Or like toys and playthings
Until their debt is paid off
Or
Until they're broken
Sick,
Used up
Then just thrown away.
Like disposable people.

—

If you don't believe that there's slavery in the world today...
Look up the State Department's report on human trafficking.[1] The 2008 report goes through human trafficking conditions and cases in country after country.

Forced exploitation of another human being's body.
Living off of the abuse of another person
Benefitting from another person's labor.
It happens. You can check out the statistics.

But after you do that, if you're able to dismiss
"Slavery" as something that happens
"over there"

Then Go to the Web site for an organization called *Not For Sale*.[2]

Click on the link for the "Slavery Map"[3]
Look at North America.
Look at the cases filed of emancipation
in Dallas
Denver
Saint Louis

Women trafficked for Sex
Sure,
But Men and children, too
for labor
In Restaurants
Households.

If you don't think that slavery happens today, then look at your shoes.

But trafficking is just part of the story.

If you don't think that slavery happens today, then look at your shoes.

Where were they made?[4]
The tomatoes with your lunch today. Where did they come from?[5]

If you have ordered off of the 99 cent value menu, purchased a $9.99 T-shirt, driven on rubber tires, or eaten a chocolate bar, then slavery that happened "over there" helped you get through your day over here.

You just didn't hear the slaves cry out.

God's people cried out.
That's what this story in Exodus tells us.
The Israelites cried out under their labor,
The author tells us,

And God heard them.

And when we hear this story
We hear it with the benefit of hindsight.
We see it through the eyes of generations of reading and hearing this story
It was the Israelites, the Hebrews—a common people—who were saved by God, led out of Egypt by Moses.

But what many scholars tell us now
Is that
The Name "Hebrew"
Evolved from another rootword:
"Apiru"[6]
A word that was used to describe
A certain class of people
It was not until generations later
That they would call themselves "Hebrew" or "Israelites"
See themselves as a nation.

At the time of the Exodus,
They weren't a common people.
The Apiru didn't see themselves
As one big happy family.
They didn't see themselves
As having an ethnic or religious identity in common.

This is what they had in common:
They were all slaves.
They were all disposable people.
And God Heard their Cry.

And turned it into a Call.

Moses heard the call.
And he had a response.

Dude, you can't mean me.
I can't go to Pharaoh.
I can't go to Nike.
I can't go to McDonald's, Taco Bell, Chipotle.
I sure can't go to the places where women and children
Are trafficked.

I know that your people are toiling
I know that they're picking tomatoes for 43 cents a bushel.[7]
I know they'd have to pick 2.5 Tons for them just to make minimum wage.[8]
I know that there are women and children sewing cargo pants and T-shirts 14 hours a day
I know they're down there on the border—in the free trade zones.[9]
Surrounded by barbed wire. I know labor laws are meaningless there.

But I can't go. Who am I? Who's going to listen to me, A shepherd?

Who's going to listen to me? A sophomore. I haven't even taken the SAT yet.

Who am I? Just a minister... This call isn't for me. I wear a robe for a living. I've got stuff to do. You know...Churchy stuff.

This is not my call.

But that's the thing: This is our call. All of us.

We're reminded of that when we hear God's name.

The translation we read here—"I am who I am"
doesn't get at the fullness of its meaning.
Some Scholars will translate it as "I will be what I will be"

With this name, YHWH, God says—when it comes to the cries of the suffering, I will act as I see fit.

I will recreate—I will rearrange the order of things

I have already chosen slaves as my people

I will turn everything you know on its head.

That is expressed in the name of the God we worship. That is our call.
She cried out to me.
"Mr. Ambassador. Mr. Ambassador!"
I suppose I could pass for an Ambassador.
The Button up shirt,
Walking up that busy Nairobi Street
Heading back to work after lunch.

I didn't usually stop for such things. But I did this time.

"You should come home with me. If you do not want me there are other girls.
Rwandan. Somali. Ugandan like me. Very reasonable price."

I can't do such a thing, I told her.

That was when she grabbed my wrist.

"Then let me come live with you.
I will work for you
I will do anything."

"I am sorry. I have no job for you."

"I will do anything."

I walked off.

Anything!

I dream of her sometimes.
It wakes me up sometimes,
and I wonder what happened to her.

But what keeps me up.
What won't let me go back to sleep on the nights I dream of her
Is that when she yelled after me

When I walked on

It was not a cry that I ignored

But a call.

Questions for Discussion and Contemplation

1 Have you heard of cases of human trafficking in your community? Is it fair to consider some of the cases mentioned in the essay "slavery"? Why or why not?

2 Can we make choices as consumers that help prevent the exploitation of workers? Does it matter?

3 What is a "coyote"? Do "coyotes" offer a service to clients or do they exploit other individuals?

Notes

Chapter 4: Thy Revolution Come

[1]Dorothy Day, *The Long Loneliness: The Autobiography of a Legendary Social Activist* (New York: Harper & Row, 1952).

[2]Gustavo Gutierrez, *We Drink from our Own Wells* (Maryknoll, N.Y.: Orbis Books, 2003), 38.

[3]Rosemary Radford Ruether, *Liberation Theology: Human Hope Confronts Christian History and American Power* (Mahwah, N.J.: Paulist Press, 1972), 190–91.

Chapter 5: Too Political for My [Clerical] Shirt

[1]Martin Luther King Jr., *The Autobiography of Martin Luther King Jr.*, ed. Clayborne Carson (New York: Intellectual Properties Management in association with Warner Books, 1998), 334.

[2]Barbara Brown Taylor, *The Preaching Life* (Cambridge, Mass.: Cowley, 1993).

[3]"Iran: Two More Executions for Homosexual Conduct" (*Human Rights Watch*, 22-11-2005), [cited 2007]. Available from http://hrw.org/english/docs/2005/11/21/iran12072.htm.

Chapter 7: *Politeuomai*

[1]Charles Gore, *The Incarnation of The Son of God: Being the Bampton Lectures for the Year 1891 (*Whitefish, Mont..: Kessinger Publishing, LLC, 2006), 185-86.

Chapter 9: Vote for My Jesus

[1]Campolo said this in an interview with Shane Claiborne titled "On Evangelicals and Interfaith Cooperation," originally published in *Cross Currents* (Spring 2005). It is also available at: http://findarticles.com/p/articles/mi_m2096/is_1_55/ai_n13798048/.

[2]David P. Gushee, *The Future of Faith in American Politics* (Waco, Tex.: Baylor University Press, 2008), 84.

[3]Interview available at: http://blog.sojo.net/2009/07/24/mark-sanford-john-ensign-and-the-family/

[4]Roger Williams and James Calvin Davis, *On Religious Liberty: Selections from the Works of Roger Williams* (Cambridge, Mass.: Belknap Press of Harvard University Press, 2008), 84.

[5]Brian D. McLaren, *A Generous Orthodoxy* (Grand Rapids, Mich.: Zondervan/Youth Specialties, 2006), 295

[6]Available at: http://blog.sojo.net/2008/07/14/advise-everyone-endorse-no-one-by-shane-claiborne/

Chapter 10: Working Two by Two

[1]Ryan Self, "Generation Y Boast Diversity", *The Optimist.* Available at http://www.acuoptimist.com/2009/09/generation-y-boasts-diversity/

Chapter 12: Defining Myself

[1]Much of these reflections are a collection and reediting of my essays for the God's Politics blog (www.GodsPolitics.com), the blog of Jim Wallis, *Sojourners,* and friends. I appreciate their permission to republish them in this form.

Chapter 13: Pulpits and Politics

[1]There's not enough room here for a conversation on how this relationship somehow does not compromise the separation of church and state!

Chapter 15: Altars, Pulpits, and Priests

[1]Full text of the speech available at http://www.nytimes.com/2008/03/18/us/politics/18text-obama.html.

[2]Luke Timothy Johnson, *The Real Jesus: The Misguided Quest for the Historical Jesus and the Truth of the Traditional Gospels* (San Francisco: Harper, 1997), viii.

Chapter 16: The Politics of Truth

[1]James H. Cone, *God of the Oppressed* (Maryknoll: Orbis Press, 1997), 15-27, passim.

[2]Edward Hooper, *The River: A Journey to the Source of HIV and AIDS* (Boston: Little, Brown and Co., 1999).

Chapter 17: Crossing to the Other Side

[1]All quotes in this essay from MetroChurch and Edmond city officials were published in the *Edmond Sun* between October 1997 and July 1998.

Chapter 19: Exodus

[1]See http://www.state.gov/g/tip/.

[2]See http://www.notforsalecampaign.org/

[3]See http://www.slaverymap.org/.

[4]See http://www.businessweek.com/magazine/content/04_38/b3900011_mz001.htm.

[5]See http://www.ciw-online.org/slavery.html.

[6]Frank S, Frick, *A Journey Through the Hebrew Scriptures* (Fort Worth: Harcourt and Brace, 1995), 260 and 272.

[7]See http://www.ciw-online.org/images/Facts_and_Figures_07.pdf.

[8] Ibid.

[9]See http://www.upenn.edu/pennpress/book/14380.html.

Volume Contributors

Vince Amlin is a graduate of the Master of Divinity program at the University of Chicago. He studied playwriting at New York University and is serving as an associate minister at a United Church of Christ congregation in Gainesville, Florida.

Kharma R. Amos currently serves as the senior pastor of the Metropolitan Community Church of Northern Virginia in Fairfax, Virginia. She received her D. Min. from Episcopal Divinity School (Cambridge, Mass.), where she focused her studies on Queering Church. Her M.Div. was awarded by Lancaster Theological Seminary (Lancaster, Pa.), where she serves as a member of the board of trustees. Kharma also serves as the chair of the Theologies Team for Metropolitan Community Churches.

David Ball is general secretary with the Student Christian Movement of Canada (SCM), a student-led ecumenical movement founded in 1921. He studied politics and journalism, and is currently involved in an Anglican (Episcopal) parish and Winnipeg Copwatch, a volunteer collective working to end police brutality. More information is at www.scmcanada.org and www.davidpball.net.

Kat Banakis is a one-time lobbyist for affordable housing and is now a postulant for ordination in the Episcopal Church. She holds a B.A. in Religious Studies and a M.Div. from Yale University.

Mary Sue Brookshire is the associate minister of the United Church of Christ of La Mesa and a charter member of the Mama Bear Alliance, a grassroots group of gay and straight parents working for marriage equality. She and her husband, Mark, stay busy parenting their twin toddlers.

Brian Dixon moved from Atlanta to San Francisco in 2003 to become the pastor of the only welcoming and affirming Baptist church in the city. He and his congregation are reenvisioning what it means to be the Church in a changing world.

Matthew Dunbar is a community organizer, social justice activist, and political commentator in New York City. He most recently held the position of director of advocacy and organizing with NY Faith & Justice and recently graduated with a master's degree in American religious pluralism from New York University's Gallatin School of Individualized Study.

John Edgerton is a graduate of the Master of Divinity program at the University of Chicago Divinity School. He is a native of Chicago and a member of Hyde Park Union Church on the city's South Side.

Earle Fisher is an adjunct instructor of religion at LeMoyne-Owen College, and is a nationally recognized and sought-after preacher, lecturer, and workshop leader. The 2008 graduate of Memphis Theological Seminary is founder of All People's House of Worship, an intergenerational, interracial, interfaith movement that promotes and participates in positive social change.

Sue Gaeta is the development director for Lutheran Volunteer Corps (LVC), a community of faith that unites people to work for peace with justice. Born in Seoul, Korea, Sue was raised in the metropolitan New York area. She received a degree in social work from Valparaiso University. She later attended Trinity Lutheran Seminary and was ordained a Lutheran pastor in 2003. She is a member of the ELCA's Congregation-based Organizing Team (CBOT) and recently finished three years of service as the president of the Gamaliel National Clergy Caucus.

Becky Garrison is a religious satirist. Her books include *Jesus Died for This?* (Zondervan, July 2010), *The New Atheist Crusaders* (Thomas Nelson, 2008), *Rising from the Ashes: Rethinking Church* (Seabury Books, 2007), and *Red and Blue God, Black and Blue Church* (Jossey Bass, 2006).

Yvonne Gilmore-Essig is presently the pastor of New Song Community Church, a church plant in Columbus, Ohio. An ordained minister of the Christian Church (Disciples of Christ) and the United Church of Christ, Yvonne is also a member of the band Cornel West Theory.

Brandon Gilvin is an ordained minister in the Christian Church (Disciples of Christ) and coeditor of the WTF? series. He is the author of *Solving the Da Vinci Code Mystery* and coauthor of *Wisdom from the Five People You Meet in Heaven*.

Amy Gopp is a preacher, poet, and peacemaker. She currently serves as the executive director for Week of Compassion, the relief, refugee, and development ministry fund of the Christian Church (Disciples of Christ).

Steve Holt is a student at Fuller Seminary working toward ordination in the Anglican Church of North America (ACNA). He currently works in Los Angeles for Clergy and Laity United for Economic Justice (CLUE).

Nicole Lamarche currently serves as the pastor of Cotuit Federated Church on Cape Cod, which is both a United Methodist and United Church of Christ congregation. She earned her M.Div. at the Pacific School of Religion and her M.A. at the Graduate Theological Union, both in Berkeley, California. Nicole is on the national planning team for the 20, 30 Clergy Network and is committed to connecting young pastors across the country.

Brad Lyons is the communications director for Higher Education & Leadership Ministries (HELM) of the Christian Church (Disciples of Christ). He and his wife, Liz, are raising their kids in St. Louis, Missouri.

Christian Piatt is the author of *Lost* (Chalice Press, 2006), *MySpace to Sacred Space* (Chalice Press, 2007), and coeditor of the WTF? book series. He cofounded Milagro Christian Church with his wife, Rev. Amy Piatt, in Pueblo, Colorado, in 2004. His blog, podcast, and other information can be found at wwwchristianpiatt.com.

Gabriel A. Salguero is the director of the Hispanic/Latino Leadership Program at Princeton Theological Seminary's Center of Continuing Education. He received his M.Div. from New Brunswick Theological Seminary and is a Ph.D. candidate in Christian Ethics at Union Theological Seminary in New York. He and his wife, Jeanette, co-pastor the multicultural Lamb's Church of the Nazarene in New York City. Rev. Salguero has been called one of the emerging voices of progressive Latino evangelicals. The Salgueros have two wonderful boys, Jon-Gabriel and Seth.

Sara Critchfield Taveras has been a social justice activist for ten years. She has a B.S. in graphic design from Drexel University and a master's in nonprofit/NGO leadership from the University of Pennsylvania. Previously she worked for the United Church of Christ's Washington, D.C. office, as a Disciples Peace Intern, and has done extensive volunteering in Central and South America. Sara currently lives in Shaker Heights, Ohio, with her life partner, Miguel.

Greg Turk has served as an urban pastor, concentrating in areas of community building and gang intervention, for fifteen years. He also serves as president of an organizational and individual performance consulting group.